D0444695

GOD'S
EXPLODING
LOVE

GOD'S
EXPLODING
LOVE

George A. Maloney, S.J.

ALBA · HOUSE   NEW · YORK

SOCIETY OF ST. PAUL, 2187 VICTORY BLVD., STATEN ISLAND, NEW YORK 10314

Library of Congress Cataloging in Publication Data

Maloney, George A., 1924 -
   God's Exploding Love

     1. God — Love.   2. Immanence of God.   3. God —
Knowableness.   I. Title.
BT140.M35   1987   231'.6   86-28802
ISBN 0-8189-0514-X

Designed, printed and bound in the United States of
America by the Fathers and Brothers of the
Society of St. Paul, 2187 Victory Boulevard,
Staten Island, New York 10314, as part of their
communications apostolate.

---

2 3 4 5 6 7 8 9 (Current Printing: first digit)

Dedication

To
Margaret Kelly
*who suggested this theme
and that I should write
this type of
book*

Acknowledgment

Sincere thanks to
Mrs. Rita Ruggiero
for typing the manuscript
and to
Sister Joseph Agnes, S.C.H.
for careful reading and correcting of the manuscript
and
for other suggestions that proved most helpful.

Table Of Contents

Introduction

The English poet, Samuel Taylor Coleridge (+1834) once wrote:

What if you slept, and what if in your sleep you dreamed, and what if in your dream you went to heaven and there plucked a strange and beautiful flower, and what if when you awoke you had the flower in your hand? Ah, what then?

Ah, what would happen if you were to be converted, as Jesus asks you, and become like a little child? What would happen if Jesus would touch your darkened eyes, open them to His loving presence within you and all around you, and give you the gift of wonderment? What would your life be like if you could wake up and not only see and rejoice at the beautiful flower and the entire material world — shimmering as moonlight with God's loving presence in your loving touch — but also see and rejoice in the Trinity as the ground of being for all creation?

Excited About God

Have you ever asked why you and I and most other Christians are not more excited about God? Why is it that, when we touch a rose, it becomes for us only a rose — and not the smiling Father, thrilling us as He did the human heart of Jesus in a loving gift of Himself to us?

I think I have the reason, at least for myself. For most Christians God is presented in church teachings and preachings as too remote, as a God "up there," a God who by nature is perfect, immutable and completely independent of all created beings. St. Thomas Aquinas teaches us that, although you and I can have a "real" relationship with God, He cannot really relate to us except by means of a "rational" relation.

Such thinking has presented us with a faulty view of God as uncaring and unconcerned about us. He really doesn't need us! But does this not deny what is found on every page of Scripture, that God has an active, concerned, involved, dynamic relationship of love for all of us? Should we believe that God's creation is a static action that occurred at the beginning of this universe and that its completion adds nothing to God's happiness but some "extrinsic" glory?

If God so loved this world, including you and me, as to give us His only begotten Son (Jn 3:16), is this not a real relationship in active, energetic, self-emptying love and not merely a "rational" one? If we take our fundamental belief that Jesus is the eternal Son of God, then, when we see Him emptied out on the cross unto the last drop of water and blood, do we not see the love of the Heavenly Father as a Suffering Servant (cf. Jn 14:9)?

This book is a humble attempt to present a new vision that really is very old. The Old Testament prophets in exile experienced this vision. Jesus taught His disciples to live in such a vision, to be transformed by God's immanent presence as out-poured love in Self-Gift just as He did. St. John, the "mystical theologian," and St. Paul experienced God as dynamic, transforming Life, living within them and inside of God's creation.

The early Greek Fathers, who theologized out of God's revelation within the Church, experienced God, as have all authentic mystics in the Christian tradition, in a knowledge that was beyond all human understanding. They discovered that the Triune God truly relates to us and all His creation as "uncreated energies of love." Grace for them primarily is God in a community of loving divine Persons, self-giving toward created "otherness." These uncreated energies of love must not be conceived as "created grace," but as God, Father, Son and Spirit, in active, energetic involvement to give themselves to us unto true communion.

World In Evolution

We modern believers have received Christianity as expressed principally in terms of Platonic and Aristotelian philosophy and Newtonian physics. Fritjof Capra, a modern nuclear physicist, describes this view of a static world:

> *From the second half of the seventeenth to the end of the nineteenth century, the mechanistic Newtonian model of the universe dominated all scientific thought. It was paralleled by the image of a monarchical God who ruled the world from above all, imposing his divine law on it. The fundamental laws of nature searched for by the scientists were thus seen as the laws of God, invariable and eternal, to which the world was subjected.*

Modern nuclear physics and astronomy with its exploration of outer space have presented a new world to us. They show us a sub-microscopic world in an energized dance toward union through interrelatedness. All things, even the subatomic particles and the "quarks," are, according to Einstein's theory of relativity, in interdependence for their uniqueness on the immediate world around them.

The entire material world is being created through events taking place in interrelated fields of energy. Our God of the 21st century has to be different for us from the God of those who lived under Newtonian physics!

A God Of Process

In our consideration of a transcendent God, actively involved in creation, we must now examine the God of process-theologians. These followers of Alfred North Whitehead reject the traditional view of God as being uninvolved in a real relationship with His creation. They show us a God who is independent and absolutely transcendent, the Possessor in His "primordial nature" of all possibilities. They highlight God's respect for our gifted free will as He "lures" us by love to co-create a better world.

We must move back in time but forward in insight to develop the faith vision of the mystics of Eastern Christianity. They add to the process theologians the mystical aspect that preserves the seeming paradox of a transcendent God who is nevertheless in vital, immanent, indwelling, energetic relations with us human beings.

The Cosmic Christ

We must turn to a modern scientist and Christian mystic, Pierre Teilhard de Chardin (+1955) whose writings combine the evolutive, dynamic world of the nuclear physicists and the mystical union with the immanent Trinity of the New Testament writers and the early Fathers of the Church.

God is found at the "heart of matter." The whole material world becomes a place of *diaphany*, or a shining through, of the risen Lord Jesus. He is the cosmic Christ as He meets us in the divine milieu of the material world around us and within us. He transforms us through His Church which becomes the "place" for us to co-create with Him the world into the total Christ of the cosmos.

An Emptying God

Yet there is something still missing in our "new" vision of God close to us as energetic, creative love. We need prayerfully to penetrate to the real essence of Jesus Christ as God's "power manifested in weakness" (2 Cor 12:9). He is the Suffering Servant of Yahweh. Now God looks like the human Jesus who emptied Himself, not of divinity, but in humanity, of all independence and non-relationship to become a servant to all the destitute.

Love is always self-emptying. It is the kenotic love of Jesus that convinces us in prayerful experience that God truly loves us (Jn 16:27). God calls us to go forth into our exploding world, unafraid, to dare more than less, to live, once His emptying love has healed us and transformed us, to become suffering servants to every man and woman, all of them our very brothers and sisters of one Heavenly Father.

Called To Freedom

Finally, we need to see what an awesome responsibility it is to know the mysteries God has revealed to us (Ep 1:9) and realize what it means to be made by God according to His own image and likeness (Gn 1:26). We are presented with obstacles preventing us from attaining the dignity of co-creators with God of this beautiful world that is "groaning" in travail all around us (Rm 8:22). This very moment reveals how much we are slaves to forces within and around us that impede our living lives of freedom in love. Yet Jesus Christ has come to set us free by releasing His Holy Spirit to lead us into a "new creation." He calls us to an inner revolution, necessary if we are to be one in co-creating a better world through love.

> *Your mind must be renewed by a spiritual revolution so that you can put on the new self that has been created in God's way in the goodness and holiness of the truth (Ep 4:23-24).*

A fitting quotation from the diary of Anne Frank, the young Jewish girl murdered by the Nazis, sums up why I have written this book. May you thrill at the *Good News* that is already alive within you and your world!

Everyone has inside himself
a piece of Good News!
The Good News is that
you really don't know
how great you can be,
how much you can love,
what you can accomplish,
what your potential is . . .
How can you top Good News like that?

George A. Maloney, S.J.

GOD'S
EXPLODING
LOVE

CHAPTER
1

A New Vision

A vast similitude interlocks all,
All spheres, grown, ungrown, small, large, suns, moons,
planets,
All distances of place however wide,
All distances of time, all inanimate forms,
All souls, all living bodies though they be ever so different,
or in different worlds,
All gaseous, watery, vegetable, mineral processes, the
fishes, the brutes,
All nations, colors, barbarisms, civilizations, languages,
All identities that have existed or may exist on this globe or
any globe,
All lives, and deaths, all of the past, present, future,
This vast similitude spans them, and always has spann'd,
And shall forever span them and compactly hold and enclose
them.

Walt Whitman
Leaves of Grass

Dr. Harold Urey, one of the inventors of the atom bomb, wrote shortly after one of the early atomic explosions on the desert flats of New Mexico: "I am trying to frighten you. I am myself a frightened man. All the experts I know are also frightened." It is reported that these experts waited for this explosion with faces to the ground. Even the most unbelieving of them felt something like a prayer rising in their hearts. It was like a prayer of a young squire on the eve of his being knighted. At that historic moment mankind ended its adolescence. We entered into our new role of master of the uncreated.

But as we learn how to split the atom and release powers that can rival the energies of the sun, we stand quivering with fright. What a power has been placed into our hands to transform the world! Or to destroy it! We cringe in our corner of this universe, afraid, feeling the need of Someone beyond us; Someone even more powerful than we are; above all, Someone who, unlike us, is totally and consistently unselfish; Someone who is Love itself.

As God created the world, He meant all parts to be coordinated into a whole, into a dancing harmony. Man and woman, alone created according to God's own image and likeness (Gn 1:26), have been given stewardship over this wonderfully rich world. God commanded us human beings:

> "Be fruitful, multiply, fill the earth and conquer it. Be masters of the fish of the sea, the birds of heaven and all living animals on the earth" . . . . God saw all He had made, and indeed it was very good (Gn 1:28-31).

This complex, multiplied world, from God's viewpoint, therefore is a unity. All creatures, through the creative inventiveness and synergism of human beings working with God's creativity in freedom, are meant to be interrelated in a harmonious wholeness. Each part has its proper place within the whole universe. Each creature depends on and gives support to all the others in one great body, all of which has been created in and through God's Word. This is described beautifully in Psalm 104:

Yahweh, what variety you have created,
arranging everything so wisely!
Earth is completely full of things you have made:
among them the vast expanse of ocean,
teeming with countless creatures,
creatures large and small . . .
You give breath, fresh life begins,
you keep renewing the world (Ps 104:24-25, 30).

This wonderful, creating God is not only the powerful, transcendent Creator who stands above and outside of all of His creation. He is also the immanent force that lives inside of every creature. "In Him we live and move and have our being" (Ac 17:28). He fills the heavens and the underworld. It is impossible to escape from His creative, sustaining Spirit (Ps 139:7).

An Old View

Our Christian faith, handed down to us from the first followers of Jesus Christ, has been given to us through a historical process of reflection. Such reflection has unfolded and has been greatly influenced by cultural factors coming out of a melting together of philosophical, scientific, theological, linguistic and mythical treasures which formed the "world-vision" of Christians of various past epochs.

Although we now are exposed to a new world-view, coming out of nuclear physics, most of us are still controlled — even in our view of God — by a Cartesian vision of "reality." We look at other persons or material objects and we think we are a separated subject, "objectively" viewing a static world of concrete, self-existent objects.

We pray to God as to another objective person. He is "above" us, outside us. Our philosophy and theology have given us certain

concepts and ideas *about* God. And we usually think these ideas are
all we can know about or experience of God.

In such a vision from classical Western Christian theology
God is pictured as complete, independent and fulfilled without any
"real" relationship with His created world, especially with human
beings.

We can give God extrinsic glory, but we cannot "affect"
Him. This is the fundamental reason, I believe, why we Christians
are not excited about God. We have objectivized the living God of
Abraham, Isaac and Jacob. God is so complete without us that He
really does not need us or even care much for us.

The Renaissance thinkers studied the material world in a truly
scientific way of deduction. This was accompanied by advances in
theoretical mathematics. Scientific experiments were described in
terms of mathematical language. Galileo is considered the father of
modern science who first combined objective observation with
mathematics.

It was René Descartes in the 17th century who believed that
the key to understanding the universe lay in discovering its logical
order. He set about to invent new mathematical forms to express
this logic of nature. All of nature, he thought, was "static" and
obedient to basic, universal laws. Descartes is perhaps most responsible for the split in the way we conceive ourselves as human
beings. He saw us as having two parts: mind and body. We were for
him a "res cogitans," a thinking thing, and also a "res extensa," a
material body. Yet his famous dictum threw the emphasis upon the
importance of the mind over the body. "Ego cogito; ergo sum,": I
think; therefore I am. We human beings are minds, caught inside a
material body that eventually will wear down through sickness and
disease and die, while we will live forever because of our "immortal soul."

Such a split within man was projected outward. All around us
exists a multitude of separated objects. It is our mind that looks at
this unchangeable world and discovers its universal laws. Man has

the power to discover eternal truths and thus to "conquer" the world of meaninglessness and fragmentation by imposing order through the mind. Isaac Newton built his mechanistic world view upon this separation of mind and matter. It was Newtonian physics that prevailed until the twentieth century, the age of nuclear physics.

Fritjof Capra well summarizes the world-view that resulted from the Cartesian and Newtonian views of man as a mind observing a static, objective world:

> *The birth of modern science was preceded and accompanied by a development of philosophical thought which led to an extreme formulation of the spirit/matter dualism. This formulation appeared in the seventeenth century in the philosophy of René Descartes who based his view of nature on a fundamental division into two separate and independent realms; that of mind* (res cogitans), *and that of matter* (res extensa). *The 'Cartesian' division allowed scientists to treat matter as dead and completely separate from themselves, and to see the material world as a multitude of different objects assembled into a huge machine. Such a mechanistic world view was held by Isaac Newton who constructed his mechanics on its basis and made it the foundation of classical physics. From the second half of the seventeenth to the end of the nineteenth century, the mechanistic Newtonian model of the universe dominated all scientific thought. It was paralleled by the image of a monarchical God who ruled the world from above all, imposing his divine law on it. The fundamental laws of nature searched for by the scientists were thus seen as the laws of God, invariable and eternal, to which the world was subjected.*[1]

Such a heavy, rationalistic framework has served to present Christianity to the West. In such a view God is static, perfect, complete and immutable. He really does not desire us or our love.

It is true that we can give Him extrinsic glory, but He is totally "unaffected" by us in His Personhood.

As we conduct ourselves toward God, so we look upon each human person and upon God's other material creations, including our very own materiality. In the Cartesian duality we are made up of distinct and separable parts of mind and body. All of us in the Western world have been brought up in such a dualistic view. Our "soul" is immortal by its very nature. Our "body" is what dies and goes into the grave. But our soul is really who we are and so after death we still live on as "soul." As Christians, we profess faith in Christ's resurrection of His earthly body and we believe we too will one day arise in our bodies from the grave.

From Plato our Western Christianity has inherited through St. Augustine such a view of the fragmentation of ourselves into separable parts. Plato strove to show the cohesion of body and soul in making us a oneness, a person. Yet, as C.A. Van Peursen points out,[2]   Plato could not put them side by side on the same plane nor could he see them as fashioning a total human being living dynamically on all levels of body, soul and spirit relationships.

For Plato, the soul is of a different order from the body. It is an entity that existed before it entered into the body. This coming together is conceived of as the result of a fall from a higher state of perfection. But it was Descartes who did more than anyone else to create the impression of the body and soul as two distinct, objective entities, existing in complete independence and isolation from each other.

Such an objectivization of the body and the soul has left its heavy mark upon our Western Christian attitudes toward sex, the material world and death itself. Sex, St. Augustine taught, is good only when it fulfills the primary end for which God meant it, namely, procreation. The secondary end, because it is rooted in matter, the source of all selfishness and sin, is mutual love between husband and wife and is not so important as the primary end.[3]

In our Western concept of death, such an inherited objectivization of body and soul has also left its heavy mark. The majority
of Christians believe that in death the body of the deceased is solely
the cadaver that is put into the earth while the soul wafts off to an
objective place called Heaven, Purgatory or Hell. At the final
resurrection our soul is supposed to zero back into the cadaver and
the individual will then be resurrected into a new body from the
dead.

Static Religion

Today we Christians are crying out for a new vision of our
relationship to God and to the world. The traditional views
presented by Western Christianity (based largely on an exhausted
scholastic philosophy and theology that came more from Plato and
Aristotle than from Christ) no longer seem adequate and meaningful in a nuclear age. Every religion has a built-in danger that allows
the faithful to settle for the trappings, the extrinsic forms of worship and dogma instead of continuing to grow through an intensive
searching into one's heart to meet the wild God of the desert who
cannot be put into convenient boxes of concepts and doctrines.
Western theology, by and large, has been reduced to a static form
of objectifying God's transcendence by separating Him in His
primary causality in all things from the created world in its
createdness.

Dr. Louis Dupré characterizes the loss of true transcendence
in theology in these words:

> From the sixteenth century on, however, reality became
> rapidly reduced to its objective, if not its physico-
> mathematical qualities. The one-sidedness of the new
> approach seriously impaired the mind's self-understanding
> and, for the same reason, its ability to conceive a genuine
> transcendence. It even reduced our view of nature. What

Heidegger writes about Descartes goes also for his successors: the world turned into a presence-at-hand (Vorhanden), *that is, an exclusive object of manipulation, closed to contemplation.*[4]

Thus today in certain theological circles there is a search for a new method, one that avoids the causal model of objective transcendence and combines in a paradoxical way God's immanence in the whole world with His awesome transcendence. God cries out to us that He is totally the Other One, so that whatever we say about Him must somehow also be denied as not totally true as affirmed.

All too often in the past, theologians advocated a "scientific" theology in which the method of theological study of Christianity was brought as closely as possible to that of the "positive" sciences. Theology from the time of the greatest Catholic theologian, St. Thomas Aquinas, in the 13th century, was considered the Queen of all sciences.

In such a theological perspective, so unlike that found in the Bible, the question about God's relationships to us and His created world is solved by declaring, as St. Thomas does, that *we* truly relate to God, but *He* cannot have a "real" relationship to us or any creature. If God were really to relate to us in our time-space slots of earthly existence, this would introduce into God's perfect transcendence an imperfection, an element of change and, therefore, of God's dependence upon us. St. Thomas writes:

God's temporal relations to creatures are in Him only because of our way of thinking of Him; but the opposite relation of creatures to Him are realities in creatures.[5]

Walter E. Stokes comments on this text of St. Thomas: "Rejection of accidental perfection is deeply rooted in St. Thomas' metaphysics of God as *esse subsistens* (as self-subsistent being) and offers no path to a new perspective from which to reconsider His relation to the world."[6] St. Thomas never remained in the abstract to prefer nature over the individual concrete person in God's personalized relationship with man. Yet Thomas' constant view of God's relations with the material, created world, including human beings, is based on Aristotle's static concepts of nature, substance and matter. The weakness of our inherited scholastic theology of the Middle Ages lies in its inability to bring God into a personalized relationship in temporality and in matter with us. St. Thomas says that God loves His creatures in the sense that He gives them good things.[7] All too often, lesser theologians than St. Thomas have pictured God as a "cosmic do-gooder", a "universal welfare agent."

Such a perspective ignores the biblical view of a Father who truly relates intimately and is completely involved with our lives. He is a God toward us as also is His image, Jesus Christ, a Man toward others. History for the Judaeo-Christian God is the "place" in time and space where He is fulfilling His Covenant in self-giving of Himself to His people. William Lynch, S.J. well explains God's relationships with our finite, material world:

> . . . if the action of God in history produces no history in God, if all the sorrow of this world does not produce an affectivity within an all-perfect God, if nothing we do can add to the fullness of Being, then we are dealing with a God who satisfies the needs of a very distinctive rationality but cannot be said to satisfy the needs of biblical reality or human beings.[8]

A Biblical Perspective

None of us can ever see God fully or know Him as He truly is. "No one has ever seen God" (1 Jn 4:12; Jn 1:18; 6:46). We would need to be God, part of His divine essence, in order to know Him fully. Only a like nature could comprehend His nature. In spite of the revelation of the Father's love made to us by His Son, Jesus

Christ, we shall never know Him fully. No matter how inflamed with His loving presence we have become, both in this life and in the life to come, there will always be something unfathomable about God. God will always absolutely transcend our human powers to possess Him completely.

Yet the good news of God's revelation, especially through His Word Incarnate, Jesus Christ, is that God in His holiness and humility wishes to share His life with us. If God is love (1 Jn 4:8), He must ''go forth'' out of Himself to be present to another, to share His being with that other. Love does not only communicate objective facts and perfections; its whole essence consists in the lover giving him/herself to another unto communion.

Thus we believe through Scripture in a God who creates the whole world in order that He might share Himself through His gifts with us human beings. Only we, amidst all other material creatures, are made ''according to the image and likeness'' of God (Gn 1:26). Only *we* are unfinished in our nature that has been gifted by God with spiritual faculties to communicate with His knowledge and to enter into communion with His trinitarian life in love. God gives us gifts and ''graces'' that are created. Yet He also relates to each human being in personalized relationships of His self-gifting to us. If God our Father counts every hair on our head (Lk 12:7), this means He is personalized and actively involved through creative love in our lives. God endows us with a share in His freedom so that we can freely take our lives and surrender them as gifts back to God.

This God is actively involved through His uncreated energies of love to meet us in the events of each moment. Hence our human nature is never static or finished. We are always in the process of *becoming* more and more our true selves in God's creative Word and His Spirit of love. Our nature can never be outside of God's loving activities. Grace is God's primary and constant presence in His creative activities in our lives, in our history. These activities cannot be separated from His nature as love. His graceful presence is inside of each event, calling us to respond to His love, but by free choices made in the context of the *now-event*.

The noted Jewish theologian, Abraham J. Heschel, points out that ours is a searching, involving God

> *He is the father of all men, not only a judge; he is a lover engaged to his people, not only a king. God stands in a passionate relationship to man. His love or anger, his mercy or disappointment is an expression of his profound participation in the History of Israel and all men.*[9]

Jesus insisted that only those could receive the Kingdom of God who had the qualities of a child (Mk 10:15; Lk 18:17). Jesus is demanding of us a conversion of heart, a becoming little and humble, receptive to God's activities in our lives. If we do not do this, the Kingdom that is before our very eyes will not be seen by us (Mt 18:3-4).

Yet such abandonment is not a reckless irresponsibility. It is the peak of acting in faith and in freedom to surrender to the loving presence of God in the *now-moment*. Such a Christian process vision finds God working in all things by His grace, His creative energies or activities of love, touching us and drawing us always into a more intimate union with Himself. It is a vision that takes us from darkness and places us fully in the light of God's loving presence as the Ground of all being. It is a true "unconcealment," an uncovering of what is always there but which our lack of faith keeps us from communicating with the ever-present and ever-loving God.

Co-Creators With God

God loves us individually and with a unique love which He manifests in different ways toward other human beings. Yet He loves His "people," all human beings created by Him in the likeness of His Son, Jesus Christ. He is affected, not only by the individual, historical Jesus, but by the Total Christ, by the human beings who keep His words and live in loving service to build a better world.

As we turn within ourselves daily in prayer and reflection that heals us of selfish love, we yield our talents to His direction. We seek to live according to God's inner harmony found in each event. We become His hands and feet, His eyes and ears. We, His servants, lovingly work to serve others. We enter the most profane situations, and yet always discover the anonymous Christ. By our involving service, especially to comfort the poor and set free the oppressed, we help in union with the risen Lord, who has received all power from His Father, to re-create this world and bring it into completion according to the plan God is conceiving out of innumerable possibilities. God waits for our cooperative consent to work synergistically with Him.

Thus the more consciously a Christian seeks to build Christ's Body through the charisms of the Spirit, the more God is becoming the loving Father of the universe. There can be no greater humanizing force in our lives than to work consciously toward this goal. We discover that we are continuously in the process — through our daily lives of activities and passivities, joys and sorrows, sin and reconciliation — of becoming divinized into God's loving children by becoming one in His only begotten Son. As we know ourselves in the Father's eternal love, we become the extension of His Son's Body, to bring others by our love and God's love in us into that Body. This is St. Paul's cosmic vision of our responsible, free cooperation with the Christ living within us:

> *And for anyone who is in Christ, there is a new creation; the old creation has gone, and now the new one is here. It is all God's work. It was God who reconciled us to himself through Christ and gave us the work of handing on this reconciliation. In other words, God in Christ was reconcil-*

ing the world to himself, not holding men's faults against them, and he has entrusted to us the news that they are reconciled. So we are ambassadors for Christ; it is as though God were appealing through us, and the appeal that we make in Christ's name is: be reconciled to God (2 Cor 5:17-20).

Not A New Vision

In our modern, impersonalized society Christians hunger to meet God immediately and directly. They are turning within to what Scripture calls the "heart," the deepest core of their being where in inner poverty and darkness they cry out to see the face of God. But they also turn outward to discover God our "fellow-Sufferer," as Alfred North Whitehead described Him.[10]

This hunger among many modern Christians to experience God in different ways than through rational positivism is not peculiar to our times. The early Christians of the East understood out of Holy Scripture that there were two ways of coming to know God: by reason and by faith. When heresies grew up in the early Church, there was need to formulate the basic truths of Christianity into defined dogmas and doctrines. Theologians developed, out of the faith knowledge given in Scripture and tradition through the teaching leaders of the Church, a *positive* theology. St. Thomas Aquina's *Summa Theologiae* is an example of positive theology called by the Greek Fathers *cataphatic theology*. It is a system of positive truths *about* God rationally deduced from observing Him in His activities toward creation. In this way, the theologian can ascribe to God certain attributes.

Experiencing God In Darkness

Yet the early Christians were very much aware from Christ's message that God could also be experienced directly and im-

mediately in a mysterious "knowledge" that was a knowing by
not-knowing. This the early Eastern Christian theologians called an
apophatic theology. We miss the richness of their approach when
we translate this as a "negative theology." We need to remove any
limitations imposed by our human reasoning about God lest we
think God really is only as we speak about Him.

The "father" of Christian mysticism, St. Gregory of Nyssa,
opened up theology in the 4th century to the positive elements of
the apophatic approach. To experience God, therefore, is not a new
need among modern Christians. It is of the essence of our Christian
faith and *praxis* that God, who is completely unknowable in His
perfect essence, can be known and experienced beyond clear and
distinct ideas through God's creative energetic working with our
creative free choices. Modern theologians call this knowledge
"pre-conceptual." It puts the stress on the actual experience of
God directly and immediately which precedes any consequent
reflection and conceptualization of what was experienced.

In St. Gregory of Nyssa's classical mystical treatise, *The Life
of Moses*, we have a full presentation of the individual Christian's
movement toward full union with God, using the analogy of
Moses' journey up Mount Sinai until he reaches God in an "understanding" that is only in the darkness of our rational, discursive
powers. The process is a stripping or a movement away from the
sensible, the reasonable, in order to meet God as invisible and
incomprehensible in the darkening of man's powers:

> *Next the soul makes progress through all these stages and
> goes on higher, and as she leaves behind all that human
> nature can attain, she enters within the secret chamber of the
> divine knowledge, and here she is cut off on all sides by the
> divine darkness. Now she leaves outside all that can be
> grasped by sense or by reason, and the only thing left for her
> contemplation is the invisible and the incomprehensible.*[11]

Mystical Theology

For the early Christian theologians, especially those of the Eastern Churches, God, the Incomprehensible One, is present and is experienced by the Christian. It is God's overwhelming transcendence that brings darkness to our own reasoning powers. The emphasis is not on the incapacity of man, but rather on the overwhelming infinity of God, always present in His creation. It is for us to seek out the fullness of God's transcendence through the experience of transcendent beauty in His creation.

Presence and transcendence are one in apophatic theology. The true contemplative is the true theologian, as the 4th century mystic Evagrius insists: "If you pray, you will be a theologian; and if you are theologian you will pray."[12] The contemplative and true theologian is the one who is given *theognosis*, knowledge about God by God, directly in an experiential intuition. Such a person, who experiences in a knowing by not-knowing through one's rational powers, breaks through the seeming paradox, that as one comes closer to union with God, the more blinding God becomes to our own control and rational powers. This is not a matter of the knowledge of God becoming more abstruse, but of the nature of God itself becoming more present to those who in their brokenness call upon Him to heal them of their ignorance and blindness. Those who purify their hearts shall truly see God through new spiritual eyes. This presence of God is brought about by the uncreated, dynamic, self-giving God in His creative, energetic love-activities taking place in and around us at all times in every event.

Let us now turn to modern physics in order to receive affirmation about the reality of God's dynamic presence in a world in which nothing is *static*. In nuclear physics we discover that everything material, possessing *mass* or quantity, is simultaneously *energy*. Such energy fields are in continuous and dynamic interacting relationships with each other.

From the great physicists we novices can accept the reality
that all created matter is moving in harmony, in a unified field of
energy that is continually being transformed from a lower level of
complexity in unity to greater levels of consciousness in oneness.

ENDNOTES

1 Fritjof Capra: *The Tao of Physics* (Berkeley: Shambhala, 1975), p. 22.
2 C.A. Van Peursen: *Body, Soul, Spirit: A Survey of the Body-Mind Problem* (London: Oxford Univ. Press, 1966), p. 35.
3 Cf.: J. Noonan, Jr.: *Contraception* (Cambridge, MA: Harvard Univ. Press, 1965), p. 137.
4 Louis Dupré: "Transcendence and Immanence as Theological Categories," In: *Proceedings of the 31st Annual Convention of the Catholic Theological Society of America*, 31 (1976), pp. 1-10.
5 St. Thomas Aquinas: *Summa Theologiae*; Prima Pars, 13, 7 ad 4.
6 Walter E. Stokes: "Whiteheadian Reflection on God's Relation to World," in: E.H. Cousins, ed.: *Process Theology: Basic Writings* (N.Y.: Newman Press, 1971).
7 St. Thomas Aquinas: *Summa Theologiae* I. q.20, 2-4; *Summa Contra Gentes*; I, 91, 2 & 12.
8 William Lynch, S.J.: *Images of Faith* (Notre Dame, IN: Ave Maria, 1973), p. 150.
9 A.J. Heschel: *Man Is Not Alone* (N.Y.: Harper & Row, 1951), p. 244.
10 A.N. Whitehead: *Process and Reality* (N.Y.: Macmillan, 1929), p. 532.
11 St. Gregory of Nyssa: *Commentary on the Song of Songs*: PG 44, 1000D, quoted from: *From Glory to Glory*, ed. by J. Danielou and H. Musurillo (N.Y.: Scribner, 1961), p. 247.
12 Evagrius: *Chapters on Prayer*; tr. by John Eudes Bamberger, OCSO (Spencer, MA: Cistercian Publications, 1970), pp. 60 & 65.

CHAPTER

2

An Exploding Universe

Have you ever thought of the great privilege you have of living at the end of the twentieth century and at the beginning of a new millennium? The discoveries alone in astronomy and space technology stagger our minds as to what discoveries await us as we explore the universe. Nuclear physicists also take our breath away with their ability to release, in the splitting of subatomic particles by bombardment, energies capable of transforming or obliterating our entire world.

Such power and magnitude locked inside of creation — but revealed to us through modern science — should give us a more dynamic experience of God as Creator of such a magnificent universe. We should be able to come closer to this loving God — who made us in His image (Gn 1:26) — as we discover His energizing love at the heart of all matter.

The Newtonian God — a static, objectivized, law-making Deity who relates to creation through His absolute laws embedded in it — is being replaced by a new vision of God and the world. Modern science helps us to break through our former ideas about God, about ourselves, about our interrelationships with other human beings and the entire created world. It allows us to move into an exciting, exploding world in which God is creatively evolving the *thisness* of each creature in a *synergy* of working with His human creatures in the process of building this world.

A New World

This is brought out in a statement of Niels Bohr, the outstanding Danish physicist:

> *The great extension of our experience in recent years has brought to light the insufficiency of our simple mechanical conceptions and, as a consequence, has shaken the foundation on which the customary interpretation of observation was based.* [1]

If St. Ignatius of Loyola could look up into the heavens and fall into ecstasy as he pondered the stars above, what should be our new concept of God as awesome Transcendence and infinite Power?

We are terrified by the enormous destructive power of the atomic bomb, which is equal to the force supplied by tens of thousands of tons of TNT, and by which Hiroshima and Nagasaki were almost completely destroyed. We are even more terrified by the power of the hydrogen bomb, which is measured by the force of millions of tons of TNT, and by which whole nations — even the earth itself — could be destroyed.

But have you ever stopped to think that these bombs are but small sparks compared with the power of the sun, of the stars and of the universe? And all these are as nothing compared with the infinite power of God!

According to recent scientific theory the energy of the sun is produced by the same process, the transmutation of matter — hydrogen into helium — as the force of the hydrogen bomb. But to make a hydrogen bomb only a few pounds of hydrogen are required. In the sun, it is said, five million tons of matter are consumed every second. This would be the equivalent, not of one or ten or a hundred or a thousand or even a million hydrogen bombs, but of tens of millions of such bombs — even hundreds of millions — exploding every second!

Further, there is enough material in the sun to produce explosions at this rate and undiminished in strength, for thirty-five billion years. If you can imagine the continual explosion of more than one hundred million hydrogen bombs per second for thirty-five billion years, you will have some idea of the great and tremendous power of the sun. But you will still have no idea of the power of God.

Now step outside and take a long look at the night sky. On a clear night you can see thousands of stars. And there are millions, even billions, more that you cannot see. In our galaxy there are approximately one hundred billion stars, and they are all generating power comparable to the power of the sun. In fact, many of them are far more powerful than the sun, which is only a medium size star. For example, there is the star Betelgeuse in the constellation Orion, which is large enough to contain thirty million suns. And the star Antares has a diameter 120 times the size of Betelgeuse. The diameter of this one star, Antares, is three times the distance from the earth to the sun.

If you can imagine the power of billions of such stars, each exploding hydrogen bombs at rates ranging from tens of millions to millions of millions of bombs per second, you will have some idea of the great and tremendous power of our galaxy. But still you would have no idea of the far greater power — the infinite power — of God.

Dizziness Of Infinite Space

Now realize that our galaxy is only one of many galaxies of stars. Outside of our own galaxy, man has actually photographed two million nebulae or star masses. And nobody knows how many of these visible masses of stars are galaxies comparable to our own, or how many masses and galaxies there may be, which have not been seen or photographed. Moreover, the distance between stars is so great that it can be measured only by the speed of light, which travels at the rate of almost six trillion miles a year. Within the galaxies stars are separated by as much as thousands, even hundreds of thousands of light-years, and the galaxies themselves are separated by distances that are not even conceivable — millions of light years, or a distance in miles equal to millions of trillions.

If you can imagine the power of millions of such galaxies, each containing billions of stars, many perhaps larger than even Betelgeuse or Antares, and each, like the sun, generating power at a rate equivalent to the explosion of hundreds of millions of hydrogen bombs per second, you will have some idea of what you are looking at when you gaze into the night sky. You will have an idea of what you cannot even see, but you will still have no adequate idea of the power of God, which is infinite and which you also cannot see.

No wonder the Psalmist could pray as he looked up into the heavens: "By the word of Yahweh the heavens were made, their whole array by the breath of his mouth" (Ps 33:6). With the Psalmist and all the mystics down through the ages, you, too, can realize that it is God's immanent power, His "insideness" in His material creation which started all these stars burring. He created the extremely high temperatures required to induce and carry on the process of nuclear fusion in these innumerable, tremendous sources of power. It is God alone who creates matter which is being consumed (or better, transmuted) at such fantastic rates into new creation.

You, too, can be convinced as were the mystics who through faith and transcendent experiences understood that God considers all this as nothing compared to you. He has placed all this powerful created universe into your hands to assist Him to co-create it into a new creation. God creates the whole world as good, as a sign of His burning desire to give Himself in faithful communication through His Word. The entire world at its interior is filled with the self-communicating Trinity. God is filling the universe with His loving Self. His uncreated energies whirl through and fill all creatures with His loving, creative presence. "He spoke, and it was created; he commanded and there it stood" (Ps 33:9).

The Dignity Of Human Beings

The created world includes not only stars and moons and suns and planets but also seas and rivers, mountains and plains, birds, animals and fishes which tumble from the finger tips of God, the Supreme Artist. He places them all in the hands of us human beings. For among all God's creatures, we alone are made according to His own image and likeness:

> *"Be fruitful, multiply, fill the earth and conquer it. Be masters of the fish of the sea, the birds of heaven and all living animals on the earth"* . . . . *God saw all he had made, and indeed it was very good (Gn 1:28-31).*

God sees this world, therefore, as a unity. All parts are meant to be coordinated into a whole, into a dancing harmony. All creatures, through the creative inventiveness and synergism of us human beings working with God, were meant to be interrelated in a harmonious wholeness. Each part has its proper place within the universe. Each creature depends on and gives support to all the others in one great whole, in one great body, all of which is being created in and through God's Word.

T.S. Eliot beautifully describes God's eternal life as the source of all created life, as a dance at the still point:

> *At the still point of the turning world. Neither flesh nor fleshless;*

Neither from nor towards; at the still point,
    there the dance is.
But neither arrest nor movement. And do not call it fixity.
Where past and future are gathered. Neither movement from
    nor towards,
Neither ascent nor decline. Except for the point,
    the still point,
There would be no dance, and there is only the dance.
I can only say, there we have been; but I cannot say where.
And I cannot say, how long, for that is to place it in time.

                                        (*Burnt Norton*)

We may consider ourselves, at least at certain times, as being weak, a seemingly lone and insignificant creature as we face such an amazing display of power, energy and beauty in the created world, in the heavens and on earth. But we must believe in God's revelation that He values not only you but each human being, more highly than all of these stars with their equivalents in hydrogen bombs and their billions of years of life. The most lowly, most abject, most uneducated, most ignorant, most degenerate human being is loved infinitely more by God than He loves all His galaxies in the night sky.

Our response ought to be the same as the Psalmist:

I look up at your heavens, made by your fingers,
at the moon and stars you set in place —
ah, what is man that you should spare a thought for him,
the son of man that you should care for him?

Yet you have made him little less than a god,
you have crowned him with glory and splendor,
made him Lord over the work of your hands,
set all things under his feet. . . .

Yahweh, our Lord,
how great your name throughout the earth! (Ps 8:3-6, 9).

This wonderful, mighty community of God, Father, Son and Holy Spirit, loves us and wishes to cooperate with our creative powers to develop this universe into a oneness that will be unto our unceasing happiness and our sharing in God's own power and love. God loves us all and wishes us to share, to be participators, in His divine nature (2 P 1:4). He will live, not for a billion years like the stars, but forever, in timeless love.

A Microcosm Of The Universe

Many of us still habitually feel that we are pitted against the sub-human world. We are given the created world to use properly. But after we die, we think we will go to "Heaven" and leave the material world behind, since we believe matter will eventually be destroyed.

On the contrary, we can never be separated from this gigantic universe. We are forever intertwined with it. This is the way God creates the stars and the oceans, the animals and us human beings.

We are a part of God's whole creation. We are more than a microcosm of the macrocosm. We are a *hologram* — that is, a part of an image that, when illumined by a laser beam, seems suspended in three-dimensional space and as a piece contains the entire image.

We are the consciousness, the love-spark that can ignite the whole and lead the entire universe with God's graceful power into a unity of diversity. Our very bodies are made up of the same matter that makes up the stars. We find the same calcium in our bodies which is found in the sea.

We have the power to "enspirit" the matter of the universe, not only into ourselves but into a unity of one body — that of the total Christ in whom "all things were created in the heavens and on the earth" (Col 1:16).

George Leonard, former senior editor of *Look* magazine, writes of our oneness with the entire material world, but from a scientific viewpoint:

*At the heart of each of us, whatever our imperfections, there
exists a silent pulse of perfect rhythm, a complex of wave
forms and resonances, which is absolutely individual and
unique, and which connects us to everything in the universe.
The act of getting in touch with this pulse can transform our
personal experience and in some way alter the world around
us.*[2]

The science of the macrocosm leads us into a great sense of
God's power and majesty. We quake before a universe that is
beyond our control, that blows apart our concepts of linear time and
space. But modern nuclear physics leads us into a new vision of
ourselves, of God, and of His world by allowing us to enter into the
world of sub-atomic particles.

Here we leave the world of mechanistic, static objects, independent of each other and of the scientific observer. We enter into
the world of mystery and interrelatedness. Everything is in flux, in
relationships.

God is energizing Love, bombarding all of His creation from
inside as well as from outside. He should no longer be conceived by
us as a God up there or over there, but as a personalized energy of
love interacting with all His creatures. He leads the universal
dance of all things in harmonious yet individualized motion,
stretching toward greater complexity and yet greater union in
multiplicity.

Let us be led into this fascinating sub-microscopic world to
understand the macrocosm and to relate more intimately with the
God of relationships.

Entering Into A New World

The world of Newtonian physics has exploded out of its static
view of reality through the exacting experiments of modern nuclear
physicists. Most of us accepted the Newtonian world as the true,

objective view of the universe. This view held sway from the second half of the seventeenth century to the end of the nineteenth. Not only natural scientists but teachers of humanities and social sciences, medical doctors, philosophers and theologians used such a vision as the true explanation of the world 'out there.''

In this Newtonian universe God was ''up there,'' an observer of a mechanical world. He directed the world through the laws of mechanics He built into it. It was constructed on the three-dimensional space of Euclidean geometry. ''Out there'' existed as an absolute space, an "empty container" in which all physical phenomena occurred.

All changes were described in terms of another absolute called *time*. Like space, it had no connection with material objects. It flowed independently from the past through the present to the future.

What moved through absolute space and time were material particles called atoms: small, solid and indestructible things. All material objects were made out of such "primary" building blocks.

The Theory Of Relativity

In 1905 Albert Einstein published his special theory of relativity and "slew a beautiful theory with an ugly fact," in the words of T.H. Huxley. Einstein proved that Newton's absolute space can no longer be considered as an independent absolute. Both space and time are interrelated and form a fourth-dimensional continuum which physicists today, using Einstein's term, call ''space-time,'' to show that all reality is relational.

In his well-known formula, Einstein shows that mass in any material object has nothing to do with a solid, independent substance but is rather a form of energy. Now energy and mass are interchangeable and inseparable. $E=Mc^2$ means that the energy of a given event is measured by the mass times the "constant" squared. For Einstein the invariable in every relative observation is the speed of light, 186,000 miles per second.

Einstein showed, therefore, that man is not a detached observer but a participator. Energy rearranges itself in new forms by creating new relationships with the surrounding environment in which it is released. The constant, regardless of space and time or the position and velocity of the observer, will always be measured by the speed of light.

Fritjof Capra illustrates the theory of relativity by pointing out that an astronomer never looks at the universe in its present state but always looks back into the past. It takes eight minutes for light to travel from the sun to the earth. Therefore, according to Einstein's theory, we see the sun as it was eight minutes ago. We see the nearest star as it existed four years ago and with powerful telescopes we see galaxies as they existed millions of years ago![3]

Now the concepts of space and time are only elements of a language used by an observer to describe an environment in which he is vitally a part. No scientist can be ''detached'' and impervious to the environment he is observing. He is a part of the whole. He uses language to describe a part of reality, but never the full reality. The scientist is both actor and spectator — in a word, an active participator in changing relationships between himself and what he is measuring or observing. John A. Wheeler insists: ''To describe what has happened, one has to cross out that old word 'observer' and put in its place the new word 'participator.` In some strange sense the universe is a participatory universe.''[4]

The Quantum Theory

In the southwest corner of Switzerland, near the French frontier, is found one of the largest machines ever built by man. It is a particle accelerator that stretches for over four miles, a maze of tunnels like a huge horseshoe which houses a thin steel pipe encased in magnets. It has the capability of producing temperatures as high as 7,000 trillion degrees Celsius, comparable to conditions an instant after the superhot explosion that created the universe itself.[5]

This underground laboratory, operated by CERN (The European Laboratory for Particle Physics), is one of ten such accelerators in operation in the USA, Europe, Japan and the Soviet Union. In all of them nuclear physicists are probing the subatomic particles that make up the atoms in our bodies as well as the same that make up the stars. The magnets guide a stream of protons around the beam line at nearly the speed of light (186,282 miles per second) before they collide with a beam of antiprotons whirling in the opposite direction. When they impact, the collision is so violent that energy is transformed into matter, creating subatomic particles that fly chaotically in all directions. Most of these released particles have a short life-span, lasting sometimes only a trillionth of a trillionth of a second before disappearing.

For the past fifty years, scientists have been exploring the atom's interior and have already solved many mysteries of matter and energy. Building on Einstein's special theory of relativity, quantum physicists pushed the discovery of Sir J.J. Thompson in 1896 of the electron to unfold energy packets called "quanta." Max Planck in 1900 showed that energy in nature was not smooth and continuous, but "lumpy and bumpy."

No one has ever seen the internal structure of an atom. If the atom is infinitesimal with our human breath containing a trillion, trillion atoms, the subatomic particles are even smaller. Within the center or nucleus are the protons which carry a positive electric charge. Neutrons are also clustered within the nucleus and are electrically neutral. Dancing in orbit around the nucleus is the third subatomic particle, the electron which carries a negative charge.

The Age Of Quarks

Quantum physicists discovered a strange characteristic of the whirling electrons around the nucleus of an atom. Unlike planets that revolve around the sun in a neatly defined orbit, electrons have no fixed paths. In fact, they act sometimes like waves and not particles. This would explain the randomness of so much of sub-atomic activity.

Physicists around the world in specially constructed cyclotrons uncovered new particles in the subatomic world. Relentlessly they sought to find the ultimate basic unit of matter, that from which all reality has its being. Einstein, until his dying day, resisted the thinking of such physicists that randomness could be the ultimate reality.

And yet as these scientists probed deeper, they came closer to harmonizing the findings of Einstein's theory of relativity with their "quanta" chaos and seeming disorder. Murray Gel-Mann in 1963 discovered that the more than 200 subatomic particles were made up of three smaller building blocks. These he called "quarks" which he discovered in James Joyce's *Finnegans Wake* in the line: "Three quarks for Muster Mark!" Strangely enough, there were three of them in the proton.

But the quarks could not be defined by any relative position or peculiar pattern of activity. They were distinguished by their properties, especially the degree of electric charge they carried. Now the theory of relativity shines through the language used by quantum physicists to describe the qualities of these quarks. As human consciousness can never be separated from the material world around it, the language of human qualities and relationships becomes the language of physicists now in the nuclear age.

The human observer was involved in subatomic particles and their activities. Contrasts and similarities produced "human" terms for the discovered five quarks as the basic units of all matter: "up," "down," "strange," "charm," and "beauty." As quarks come in pairs, physicists believe there should be a sixth quark which will pair up with "beauty" and will be called "truth." This highlights Einstein's theory of relativity and suggests through such human qualities given to quarks that the "perceptual unit" of us human beings and "it" are parts of the basic structure of all matter. Human consciousness is involved in the creation of the world, and the material world helps form human consciousness. We are dealing with fields of force and energy and no longer with solid entities. Molecules whose electrons generate a force in one area like a magnet affect us, the "outsiders," who really can never be outside of the material world around us.

A Network Of Interrelationships

We see now that the material world around us and within the microcosm of our bodies exists — or better, is being created and is evolving — through complex events of energy-interrelationships. F. Capra well describes what the quantum theory leads us to as a new vision of the universe and our interrelationships with each part of the whole:

> *Quantum theory forces us to see the universe not as a collection of physical objects, but rather as a complicated web of relations between the various parts of a unified whole. This, however, is the way in which Eastern mystics have experienced the world, and some of them have expressed their experience in words which are almost identical with those used by atomic physicists.*[6]

In all religions that have maintained a mystical view of the immanence of a personalized divinity inside of all created things, to experience the unity of all diverse creatures in the Absolute One is the goal of human wisdom. A world of separated objects is considered in such mystical traditions as an illusion created by man's rational powers. Inner discipline, especially through transcendental meditation of the "insideness" of the Divine One, leads us out of what Hinduism calls "maya" or a state of living in darkness, illusion and unreality.

Today many quantum physicists speak in terms of the interrelationships of all things to each other, and the unity of all in a wholeness, that resembles the language of mystics. Einstein wrote the following statement because he had experienced through his experiments and insights that religion without science is impossible and science without religion was incomplete:

> *The most beautiful and most profound emotion we can experience is the sensation of the mystical. It is the sower of all true science. He to whom this emotion is a stranger, who can no longer wonder and stand rapt in awe, is as good as dead. To know that what is impenetrable to us really exists, manifesting itself as the highest wisdom and the most radiant beauty which our dull faculties can comprehend only in their most primitive forms — this knowledge, this feeling is at the center of true religiousness.*[7]

Mysticism:
The Experience Of Oneness In All Things

Mysticism moves beyond the Cartesian duality of subject and object. In this there is a very great similarity between both the language of mystics and quantum physicists and the actual experience they both undergo as they penetrate beyond the outside shell of the physical, sense world.

Evelyn Underhill, an English expert on mysticism, gives us an apt description of it that could have been written by Einstein or several other modern physicists:

Mysticism is the expression of the innate yearning of the human spirit towards total harmony with the transcendental order, whatever may be the theological formula in which this order is expressed. This yearning with the great mystics gradually takes possession of the whole field of consciousness; it dominates their whole life and attains its climax in that experience called mystic union, whether it be with God or Christianity, the World soul of pantheism or the Absolute of philosophy. This desire for union and straining towards it in as much as they are vital and real (not purely speculative) constitute the real subject of mysticism. Through this the human consciousness reaches its further and richest development.[8]

Today modern physicists no longer see a severe dichotomy or separation between the spiritual and the physical. Quantum physics has clearly shown that not only do our human mind and consciousness affect the experiment or the physical environment, but that they are also affected. Dr. Larry Dossey writes: "Perhaps the spiritual goal of transcending the physical can be rethought. Our greatest spiritual achievement may lie in total integration of the spiritual and the physical — in realizing that the spiritual and physical are not two aspects of ourselves, but one. Perhaps the ultimate spiritual goal is to transcend *nothing*, but to realize the oneness of our own being. . . ."[9]

The Hindu Upanishads describe God in a non-separable manner from the material environment:

He is down there, He is here, quite close. He is within all that is; from all that is. He is apart. He is everywhere shining, bodiless without limbs, seeing, wise, born of Himself. He it is who orders everything aright throughout the eternal years.

The Isha Upanishad proclaims the All-in-Allness of God within the material universe:

Plenitude everywhere; Plenitude there, here. From Plenitude comes forth Plenitude and everywhere one with itself there remains Plenitude.

Non-Duality

For the Western mind good is opposed to bad, birth to death, the finite to the infinite. But to oppose God as infinite to everything else as finite is to set up a false duality. God's plenitude cannot be placed within an oppositional duality. The Hindu *Advaita* or non-duality is a theological statement that flows out of an indepth experience of God as the ocean of being in which man floats as a drop. It preserves the mystery that cannot be unraveled through an intellectual process but which can be approached only in the darkness of paradoxes. The Upanishads express this mystery: "He is not known by him who knows Him, not understood by him who understands. He alone contemplates Him who has ceased to contemplate Him. In all knowledge as though by intuition, the wise man finds Him. It is in Him alone, the *Atman*, that each one is strong. It is in knowing Him alone that one becomes immortal. A great loss it is, in truth, for him who does not attain Him here below."

For the Far Eastern or Eastern Christian contemplative to explain the union of God and man and the material world by any limiting concepts is to mock the real experience. And yet any contemplative, from either the East or the West, knows from experience, once he/she has entered into the interior castle, that God is never an object to be looked at and petitioned, to be controlled by one's intellect in cold objectivity. God is experienced as present to the contemplative as breath is in the breather.

Enlightenment

We cannot live in relationships to our material world, to God, to ourselves and to other human beings according to the classical framework that evolved in the Western world through Aristotle and Newton. Such a vision denies holism, the sense of the unity of all beings and the mutual belonging to each other through dependent, interacting relationships.

This has been the teaching of all religions that have maintained the non-classical, mystical tradition. Enlightenment or *samadhi* comes when one breaks through the binding grip of the filter system of human discursive thought that prevents one from entering into the dynamic environment of energies and material creatures to come to experience the oneness of all things in the Absolute One:

> *Entering into the* samadhi *of purity, (one obtains) all penetrating insight that enables one to become conscious of the absolute oneness of the universe.*[10]

Perhaps Einstein's conviction should become ours: "Science without religion is lame; religion without science is blind."[11]

ENDNOTES

1 Niels Bohr, cited by Fritjof Capra: *The Tao of Physics* (Berkeley, CA: Shambhala, 1975), p. 54.
2 George Leonard: *The Silent Pulse* (N.Y.: Bantam New Age Books, 1978), Preface; xii.
3 F. Capra, p. 169.
4 J.A. Wheeler, cited by F. Capra, p. 141.
5 See the article by John Boslough: "Worlds within the Atom," in *National Geographic*: Vol. 167; no. 5 (May 1, 1985; pp. 634-660).
6 F. Capra, p. 138.
7 Albert Einstein as quoted by Lincoln Barnett: *The Universe and Dr. Einstein* (N.Y.: New American Library, 1962), p. 108.
8 Evelyn Underhill: *The School of Charity and the Mystery of Sacrifice* (N.Y.: Longmans, Green & Co., 1956), p. 235.
9 Dr. Larry Dossey: *Space, Time & Medicine* (Boulder, CO & London: Shambhala, 1982), p. 197.
10 F. Capra, Ch. 10; fn. 2.
11 A. Einstein: *Ideas and Opinions*, cited by Edgar Mitchell: *Psychic Exploration. A Challenge for Science* (N.Y.: Capricorn, 1976), p. 13.

3

God In Process

We moderns are preoccupied with two fundamental problems which are actually connected. We worry whether a nuclear war will blow us and our entire world into annihilation. On the other hand, we hungrily seek for greater meaningfulness in our human existence. We passionately want wings that will lift us high above the mundane, the sordid, to possess the unpossessable Beauty, Goodness and Love whom we call the transcendent God.

The burning question among modern theologians and philosophers is: How can we encounter God in a world that is evolving so rapidly? Better yet, the greater question is: How does God relate to us in the context of our modern living? As we change in our conscious awareness of ourselves through more personalized relationships with others and with an exploding universe around us, so our understanding of our traditional religious symbols and ways of conceiving God change.

A New Vision Of God

We have already described the traditional, classical, theistic view of God developed in 13th century scholastic theology and confirmed by 17th century Newtonian physics. Walter Stokes asks the question: "Can God's love for this world be more adequately expressed than it has been in the traditional theistic position which holds that God's knowledge and love of this world involves in Him nothing more than a rational relation?"[1]

Let us investigate the vision of God and His creation as presented by what are called "process-theologians."[2] Such thinkers usually base their world-view on the process-thinking of Alfred North Whitehead, without excluding influences from the existential and evolutive views of Martin Heidegger, Henri Bergson, Maurice Blondel and Pierre Teilhard de Chardin. Through the strengths and weaknesses of such insights, we can be in a better position to appreciate a theology of God's uncreated energies as found in Scripture and in the theological writings of some of the leading Eastern Christian Fathers.

Process-philosophy thinkers maintain that their discovery opens for Christian theology a way of conceiving God in historical-temporal terms. It seeks the "logos" of being:

> *The biblical God acts in a history where men have freedom which they can misuse. He is at work in time, and it is just this which the theological tradition, conditioned by neoplatonic metaphysics has never been able to encompass.*[3]

The first and perhaps basic assumption of Whitehead and process thinkers in general is that the world is a dynamic rather than a static reality. Human nature, for example, cannot be described as an immutable and unchanging thing. Man is a living, changing, developing creature. Likewise, the world of nature is not something static:

> *Down to the lowest levels of matter, if we may so style them, this capacity for and presence of change and development is to be seen.*[4]

A World Of Becoming

Process thinkers take seriously what nuclear physicists tell us about the created world of matter. They point out to us the dynamic, living, evolutionary quality of our existence and of the world in which we live. It is a world in flux, never statically fixed in self-contained entities of *being*. Everything and everyone, including God, is in interrelational "events" of *becoming*. The world as a whole is both in process and is itself a process.

This leads to a second assumption which is basic to process thought. The World and all that is in it is an interrelated society of "occasions." There is no possibility of isolating one occasion from another so that each may be considered in itself alone. Into each given occasion there enter past events as well as present pressures and the "lure" of the future. A man, for example, cannot exist in complete isolation from other people, or from his own past history, or from any of the developments of mankind in general. In being "himself," he is all that has gone on within him and around him:

> We live in and we are confronted by a richly inter-connected, inter-related, inter-penetrative series of events, just as we ourselves are such a series of events.[5]

In process thought, as Whitehead develops it, there is given to us a variety of relationships which have played upon us and have brought about what in fact we experience. The converging process brings *this* rather than *that* to a focus. What in older philosophy might have been seen as a chain of cause and effect is seen in a much richer understanding of occasions, pressures, movements and events which come to focus at *this* or *that* point.

For Whitehead, the thing which secures the identity of each particular occasion is its "subjective aim" which is proper to each series of occasions. There is an element of teleological concern in all process thought. This does not mean that this aim is conscious in each set of occasions (an acorn is certainly not aware of the "aim" which keeps it moving in its proper development), but what does keep things moving is the subjective aim which they possess. A consequence of these assumptions is the rejection of all those dualisms which would make simple divisions between mind and matter, nature and supernature, etc.

Understanding Of God

Now let us look briefly at Whitehead's understanding of God. Whitehead has a close affinity to the classical metaphysical tradition. He wishes to maintain the eternal order in the mind of God, but he also wants to conceive a reality which includes God as having a real history of concrete happenings.

Whitehead and those theologians who interpret his thinking have a great difficulty with what they understand to be traditional theology. Whitehead's most telling statement against the tradition is that "the Church gave God the attributes which belonged exclusively to Caesar."[6]

Theologians like Schubert Ogden argue that this traditional view of God has alienated modern man. For process theologians:

> *The whole character of traditional theism is defined by an essential one-sidedness or monopolarity. As it conceives God, he is so far from being the eminently relative One that he is denied to be really related to our life at all.*[7]

In other words, God's relations with the world are purely external, of a transcendent objective nature, totally lacking any immanent relationship.

Process thinkers will admit that traditional theology does speak of God as having real relationships with His creation. God freely creates and judges all things and by His mercy brings everything to its final end. But this is seen as nothing more than a mere appearance.

In the final analysis according to process-thinking, conceiving God as the Absolute of classical, scholastic philosophy is absolutely repugnant to anyone who has a truly secular attitude toward life in this world. Since God is wholly absolute, nothing whatever can make the least difference to Him:

> *God's perfection is in every sense statically complete, an absolute maximum, so we can no more increase Him by our best efforts than diminish him by our worst.*[8]

Infinite Possibilities In God

According to Whitehead's main outline of his doctrine of God, there are two aspects of the divine nature. The first he calls the *primordial nature* of God. This is the ordered realm in which is found all the possibilities of values and meanings that are relevant to existence. Whitehead holds that this side of God's being does not change. It is present to Him in one perfect vision. For Whitehead, this aspect of God's nature has all the attributes which have been traditionally assigned to Him. Since it is eternal, it cannot be acted upon or suffer. If there is a meaningful world in process, there must be something which sets the boundaries of how things can be related to one another.

Consequent Nature

For Whitehead, however, there is another aspect of God which he calls *consequent nature*. God's actuality involves concrete process. God shares with His creatures a degree of freedom so that His interaction with His creatures involves real intercommunication. What happens in the world is of concern to God. He responds concretely to every new event by taking it as a datum into a new phase of His own life and arranging it according to His vision. What remains fixed for God is the integrity of His aim which looks toward the fullness of life for the whole of creation.

It must be pointed out clearly that Whitehead does not identify God with the world process. Rather, He is the eternal structure which makes the world possible in the first place and which participates in each moment of the world's becoming. God is a conscious, personal being.

God is the one who gives an ordered pattern to the creative life of the world to bring new possibilities into existence. God holds the world together by offering His eternal structure to everything that happens and brings it in relation with the whole community of beings. God, however, does not destroy the freedom of creatures within this order. For Daniel Day Williams, process theology is a significant improvement on Augustine's thought:

> *We avoid here one of the curious consequences of the Augustinian ontology which is that the world can add nothing to God. How can you add anything to absolute perfection? But in Whitehead's doctrine, every achievement of good, of value, of meaning in the world increases the richness of God's being.*[9]

Creative Freedom

In a process-view of God and His creatures, especially human beings whom He creates according to His own image and likeness (Gn 1:26), events do not happen solely by God's creative power. Out of His many possibilities God sends out to His human creatures "lures" or gentle attractions of tender love. He retains His absolute transcendence, omniscience and omnipotence. Yet within His utter independence of all creatures and His necessary being, God (as His revealed word in Scriptures assures us) shares His freedom and responsible creativity with His human children.

God is the power that actuates possibility but He does so by drawing us into the orbit of His beauty, truth and love. He gently persuades us as a friend persuades and does not coerce the beloved to a single course of action but to various possibilities that fulfill the destiny of the beloved.

In His immense humility God allows us freely to join Him in creative choices to bring this world into its fulfillment in God's Logos. All possibilities are available to us but in "graded relevance," as Whitehead describes the possibilities presented us from our free choice.

Our choices are respected by God in His loving concern for us and in His immanent presence to us through His providence. Such a providence contains first God's "aim" for each occasion. He wishes, as a loving Father, that in every event we cooperate out of faith, hope and love with Him to bring forth into actuation out of the possibilities available to us the maximum beauty, goodness and unity through love by our free choices.

We can see that providence also contains a special involving work of God to accept lovingly and respectfully our free choices and "adjust" Himself to those choices in order to "save" them as Whitehead puts it:

> *The image — and it is but an image — the image under which this operative growth of God's nature is best conceived, is that of a tender care that nothing be lost. The consequent nature of God is his judgment on the world. He saves the world as it passes into the immediacy of his own life. It is the judgment of a tenderness which loses nothing that can be saved. It is also the judgment of a wisdom which uses what in the temporal world is mere wreckage.*[10]

This is the Christian faith that St. Paul expresses — how God operates within the framework of our free choices to draw good out of our actions, even if they have been faulty or evil. "We know that in everything God works for good with those who love him, who are called according to his purpose" (Rm 8:28). Each of our human, free choices sets the stage for not only the next series of new possibilities but also of God working within those possibilities. God is truly "affected" by our choices as He adapts to our decisions. David A. Fleming comments on Whitehead's presentation of the interaction of God and man: "Man has through his own creative action opened up these new possibilities, and these new possibilities are once again ordered for man and informed with new 'lures,' new ideal aims and loving invitations of God."[11]

A God Of History

Thus in the process-view we discover a world in which God and man work synergistically to co-create an evolving world. The Psalmist stands in awe at man's freedom and responsibility which God gives to him. "What is man that thou art mindful of him, and the son of man that thou dost care for him?. . . . Thou hast given him dominion over the works of thy hands; thou hast put all things under his feet. . . ." (Ps 8:4, 6 RSV).

We human beings possess freedom and receive a call to make responsible decisions, to choose out of the many possibilities God offers us at each moment. Our human situation is, therefore, the important meeting place of the co-creativity of God and ourselves. Our decisions truly do matter, as Whitehead consistently points out. Our choices are important and have value. They impact our future decisions and even affect God's future cooperation as well as that of other human beings and sub-human creatures.

Our decisions have consequences to change the past and to direct future possibilities into actuation. How often we see in our lives the influences affecting other creatures in their movement toward greater completion!

A Cosmic Lover

Process theologians not only take seriously the cosmos as an exploding, energetic series of events that are in vital interrelationships, but they also accept the Good News of Christianity that God truly loves His world (Jn 3:16). God, therefore, freely wills to give Himself in personal love to His created children. Through His own act of self-giving, God creates man with the power to complete this gift by a free response in love.

But we human beings, in order to be related in love to God, need "to participate in God's very own nature" (2 P 1:4). We need to be more than mere material creatures, for such as these cannot be self-relating and self-gifting in response to God's love. We must be spirit-in-flesh. We are made by God to be "enspirited," materialized persons who develop in a time and space continuum.

Thus time for us (particularly our own existence in time from birth to death) is extremely important. For it is in time and space that we can respond to God's self-gift to us by our return of love to the Cosmic Lover. Our free choices, therefore, decided in our temporal history, are vitally important. They influence ourselves, the world around us, and even God.

Process theology offers us a new vision which reflects the dynamism found in God's personalized love relations with His human creatures in the history of salvation as recorded in Scripture. It shows a marked resemblance to the living theology of the early Eastern Fathers who grounded their theology, not on Aristotelian physics of an unmoved Mover, but on their own mystical experiences of God's revelation.

Process thought springs out of the views of modern physicists. The philosophers and theologians influenced by this thought open up to us a world in which God is *really* related to His created world.

Dr. Langdon Gilkey well expresses the contributions this view can make to move us out of a view of static natures that no longer seems to be expressing the reality in which we live.[12]   First, we begin to see in this new vision that God submits Himself in relation to finite beings according to the principle of divine *self-limitation*.[13]

This means that God, as Creator and Conserver of all creatures, freely wills to share His creativity in a process involving His creatures. This in no way takes away from God's transcendence, nor does it place God in a finite process of becoming. We can and do shape history through our own self-determination only because God freely wishes to share His power of creativity with us. Thus creation is a process involving the work of God in union with the freedom He creates in man.

Secondly, such process-thinking allows us to understand the humility of God who freely consents to enter into our temporality and be affected by it.[14]   This is exemplified by the Incarnation. In Christ Jesus, as in microcosmic dimensions, God consents to become "temporal" and to move and act in our temporality. This in no way makes God a creature of a time-process, for He is the ultimate, creative ground of being of all process. He is the necessary condition for each moment and is present in each moment. Yet He transcends each moment. For God, the future, according to Gilkey, is possibility and not actuality. Before the historical birth of Christ, the Incarnation for God was an event possible but not yet actualized. Different relationships in time and space were actuated and brought God into very real relationships with temporality different from His relationships to the created world before the Incarnation.

God Becomes

Gilkey gives us a third major difference in our understanding of God in a process-view.[15]   God always remains, as scholastic philosophers refer to Him, *a se*, necessary and not contingent upon any outside being, complete and transcendent as to be beyond any transient growth or developmental process. Yet God Himself "becomes" or is subject to change.[16]   We are shocked at the thought proposed that God could change, that He possesses *potency* that through a temporal process could be actuated and thus add a perfection to God.

Process-thinkers insists on the distinction between actuality and possibility. God's power of being brings about newness of being by actuating with human cooperation out of His many possibilities. God is considered by process-thinkers as vitally involved in change and process. His creative and providential relations to man and the rest of creation undergo change. God's "experience" and "knowledge" of His world change.[17]   God is "becoming" in the process of possibility becoming actuality. History changes and so does God in His freedom to continue to "save" the most of love, harmony and truth out of each event. God is absolute Transcendence and not dependent upon His creatures. Yet God freely consents to limit His possibilities as they are narrowed into actuality by man's free choices. God in process-thinking is both the beginning and the end of all reality, the ultimate Source who has no other source of His infinite perfection. Yet God cannot be, at the end of the temporal process of actuating this created world, the same as He was at the beginning.

This cursory presentation of process-thought has faced us with many bold, even seemingly shocking affirmations about God in relationship to His created, evolving world. Let us turn to Scripture and the early Eastern Fathers to present God in His loving relationships to His world. Perhaps elements or approaches missing in process-thought can be brought in to create for us a broader vision of God's dynamic, energizing, triune relationships to us and our world. "God looked at everything he had made, and he was very pleased" (Gn 1:31).

ENDNOTES

1 Walter E. Stokes: "Whiteheadian Reflection on God's Relation to World," in: E.H. Cousins, ed.; *Process Theology: Basic Writings* (N.Y.: Newman Press, 1971), p. 138.
2 The following are some key books on the topic of process-philosophy and theology. A.N. Whitehead: *Process and Reality* (N.Y.: Macmillan, 1929); Norman Pittenger: *Process Thought and Christian Faith* (N.Y.: Macmillan, 1968); Schubert Ogden: *The Reality of God* (N.Y.: Harper & Row, 1966); Harry James Cargas & Bernard Lee, ed.: *Religious Experience and Process Theology* (N.Y.: Paulist Press, 1976); Norman Pittenger: *God in Process* (London: SCM Press, 1968); *Christology Reconsidered* (London: SCM Press, 1973); *Goodness Distorted* (London: Mowbrays, 1970); E.H. Cousins, ed.: *Process Theology. Basic Writings* (N.Y.: Newman Press, 1971); B. Lee: *The Becoming of the Church* (N.Y.: Paulist Press, 1974); Charles Hartshorne: "Whitehead's Idea of God," in: *Whitehead's Philosophy* (Lincoln: Univ. of Nebraska, 1972); Daniel Day Williams: *The Spirit and the Forms of Love* (N.Y.: Harper & Row, 1968); John B. Cobb, Jr.: *The Structure of Christian Existence* (Philadelphia: Westminster Press, 1967); Peter Hamilton: *The Living God and the Modern World: Christian Theology Based on the Thought of A.N. Whitehead* (Philadelphia: United Church Press, 1967); C. Hartshorne: *Reality as Social Process: Studies in Metaphysics and Religion* (Glencoe, IL: The Free Press; and Boston: Beacon Press, 1953); Bernard E. Meland: *Faith and Culture* (N.Y.: Oxford Univ. Press, 1953); Langdon Gilkey: *Reaping the Whirlwind* (N.Y.: Seabury Press, 1976).
3 D.D. Williams, *The Spirit and the Forms of Love*, p. 107.
4 N. Pittenger: *Process Thought and Christian Faith*, p. 12.
5 Ibid., p. 13.
6 A.N. Whitehead: *Process and Reality*, p. 520.
7 S. Ogden: *The Reality of God*, p. 48.
8 Ibid., p. 51.
9 D.D. Williams, p. 109.
10 A.N. Whitehead, p. 525.
11 David A. Fleming: "God's Gift and Man's Response" in: Harry James Cargas & Bernard Lee: *Religious Experience and Process Theology*, p. 223.
12 Langdon Gilkey: *Reaping the Whirwind* (N.Y.: Seabury Press, 1976), pp. 300-317.
13 Ibid., p. 307.
14 Ibid., p. 308.
15 Ibid., p. 309.
16 Ibid.
17 Ibid.

Luminous Darkness

Karl Barth had a great love for Mozart and his music. Each day for years, he played some Mozart before writing because he hoped that such transcendent music would unconsciously awaken in him the hidden, sophianic music that comes in tune with the divine, cosmic music that saves speculative theology by an experience of the ineffable in love.[1]

Music, like theology, admits of two aspects, to quote Henri Bergson:[2] "the closed" and "the open" society. Mozart, Beethoven and all great musical composers created very systematically architectonic and elaborate symphonies. Yet hidden outside of the intellectual plane, there was a transcendent point to which the composer returned to test all his rearrangements and intellectual plans. Here was the creative spark that soared in unlimited, ethereal spaces beyond any intellectual confinement.

Perhaps by returning to the mystical insights of the early Eastern Christian Fathers — who were theologians in the positive, speculative sense, but also mystics — we can compensate for some of the inadequacies of the modern process-thinkers. These latter seemingly rebel against a closed theological system as presented by medieval scholasticism and as handed down in the "traditional theism" of Western Christianity. Their limitations, however, come in their refusal to enter into the mystical, the world of the apophatic and the mysterious. In such a faith-full world that gives us the needed reverence toward the awesomeness of God's transcendence, the "mysterium tremendum" of Rudolf Otto,[3] God is free to act independently and prior to our free choices. God does agree to work along with our free choices and reveal Himself to us in them. But He also is free — out of His infinite love, goodness and power — to take the initiative in our lives, as we see in His initial act of creation.

Process theologians have maintained God's transcendence and loving, creative involvement in our material world, but they seem in general to avoid the immanent, energizing presence of God within our very beings and the world. Their God is still "outside" of us as an object among many objects. Human intelligence can bring us just so far and then we must fall on our knees before the "cloud of unknowing."

The early Eastern Christian Fathers, especially the Greeks, were able to bring together the transcendence and the immanence of the Christian God in a more complete way than process thinkers have done. Let us turn now to learn from them about a knowledge that is experiential, yet might seem to be "unreal" and removed from the "practicality" of our material existence. Process thinkers are apparently ignorant of this process-system that came out of the mysticism of Christian love which differentiates as it unites us. This mysterious love of the Spirit exalts our freedom to respond to God's humble, serving love. Yet such love can only be experienced, since it far exceeds the boundaries imposed by all our human intellectual schemes and categories.

Eastern Christian Mysticism

Christianity was born as the flowering of Judaism. Moses was the model of Semitic mysticism: one who in awe and trembling dared not to look upon the face of Yahweh but rather listened to the Word of God and surrendered in loving obedience. Moses met God on top of Mount Sinai in the cloud of darkness amidst thunder and lightning. The accent is on the existential encounter with the Absolute through a reverent, silent listening — not in images, concepts or reasoning.

St. John's Gospel portrays the incarnate Word of God as Life, to be experienced and received, to be the new force to make us into children of God. Christ is the Life of God and is our true, full life. The early Christian writers, therefore, transmit faith, the Gospel and the sacraments under the aspects of life, not as intellectual concepts. Faith is the germ of eternal life. To preach the Gospel is to sow the word of love. To obey the Word of God is to "know the Father and him whom the Father has sent" (Jn 17:3). Salvation is a new life in Christ that has to grow and possess our consciousness more and more.

Gradually there appeared in Christianity a shift from the existential to a more intellectual approach. Origen in the 3rd century developed the Platonic concept of life assimilating light. Evagrius of Pontus, who has been described as a Christian Buddhist, defined prayer in terms of the mind: "The state of prayer is a passionless state in which supreme love transports on high a wisdom-loving spiritual mind."[4]

God is now to be seen by the intellect of man turned within. He is experienced as light in an intellectual vision. This is the doctrine of the Alexandrian School, developed largely in the mysticism of Clement of Alexandria, Origen and Evagrius of Pontus.

The more holistic, Semitic influence, with its accent on the total, existential encounter with God in the "heart," continued chiefly in the Antiochene School. Ignatius of Antioch, Polycarp, Irenaeus, Pseudo-Macarius and the Fathers of the Desert placed the accent on an affective encounter in the "heart," the core of man's being. In this encounter the individual Christian would meet Jesus as the living, healing Lord through faith, hope and love. It is the heart, not the mind, where God is encountered as the source of life. The *Jesus Prayer* would develop out of the affective heart-spirituality, not out of a spirituality of intellectualism.

By reverently pronouncing the name of Jesus, the Eastern Christian mystic in the desert was immersed in the presence of the Risen Lord. Here we encounter an existential spirituality built around a mysticism of darkness, not intellectual light. It is temerity to approach God solely by any human reasoning. It is by purification of the heart that man disposes himself to receive God's revelation of Himself as the Life-Giver. This is received, not by means of any intellectual experience, but in the darkness of the human intellect. It is this ''apophatic'' spirituality that, I believe, will open us to encounter in a personalistic relationship the uncreated energies of the hidden community of love, the Divine Trinity.

Apophatic Spirituality

The distinguishing characteristic of Eastern Christian mysticism is its apophatic quality. Like the Far Eastern variety, Eastern Christian mysticism insists that the highest union with God (the infused union, in which God speaks to us directly about Himself) is not achieved in any conceptual knowledge, but in an immediate, experiential knowledge wherein He opens Himself to us. We can never come to this knowledge through any concept, rationalization or discursive method of our own. God, purely and simply in His transcendence, reveals Himself to us when and how He wishes. After years of our own preparation and cooperation through continued purification, God sees that we are humble enough to be so open to Him as to see Him in everything and to see ourselves as an offshoot of His overflowing love. Then, in a working *synergy*, we can cooperate to co-create with God this world into a more beautiful revelation of His love.

Apophatic is usually translated as *negative*, but this is to misunderstand the nuanced mysticism of these early Fathers. The accent is entirely on God doing the revealing, giving the Gift of Himself in complete freedom. No longer is man/woman and their personal activities the place of emphasis. God the Incomprehensible, who is so infinitely perfect and good in His essence, deigns to allow us to know Him as a directly experienced Lover.

A Positive Theology

The other manner of knowing God, the *cataphatic*, is a positive assertion about God's attributes. It is used by the Eastern Fathers, but more or less as a preparation for the higher stages of knowledge through contemplation. Cataphatic theology uses the perfections that we find in creatures about us, and from this limited knowledge we are able to know something about the infinite perfections of God. St. John Damascene describes the positive approach of theology:

> *God is infinite and incomprehensible and all that is comprehensible about Him is His infinity and incomprehensibility. All that we can say cataphatically concerning God does not show forth His nature, but things that relate to His nature. God does not belong to a class of existing things. He receives no existence, but is above all existing things. If all forms of knowledge have to do with what exists, that which is above knowledge must be above all (created) essence, and what is above essence must be above knowledge.*[5]

Thus, the Fathers unanimously agree on the importance of a cataphatic or positive, deductive, affirming approach to theology. They see such an approach as yielding a certain positive knowledge about God, man and the world. But this is an imperfect way and must be complemented by the apophatic approach. The positive approach to theology is a descent from the superior degrees of being to the inferior. It is to speak of God through His causality upon the material effects of his created order, including man/ woman and the entire material world.

The Negative Way

In the Western Christian world, we exalt science and knowledge of the mind. Certain Catholic and Protestant theologians have yielded to the temptation to create an almost exclusively cataphatic theology. In the 4th century a heresy grew up in the East called *Eunomianism* which shows the dangers of a theology that cuts itself off from the apophatic and the mystical. Its founder Eunomius pushed positive theology and the ability of man to form rational concepts about God to the limit of heresy.

Eunomius held that the divine essence could be clearly known by man. It could be apprehended intellectually and exhaustively in the mere fact that one accepted the supposed revelation of God as "not engendered." Once one "saw" the truth of this postulate that the Father alone, the "not engendered," was God, one entered into the full light of the divine essence and God Himself had no more light than this.

In such a system the Son and the Holy Spirit are considered as creatures of God. Christianity becomes emptied of all mystery. We human beings can attain and apprehend all there is to know of God. By destroying the immanence of the mysterious indwelling Trinity, known only by childlike faith through God's revelation, Eunomius destroyed also the transcendence of the one God in His unknowable essence.

Against such thinking the great Cappadocian theologians and mystics, St. Basil, St. Gregory of Nazianzus and St. Gregory of Nyssa, developed an apophatic theology as a necessary corrective. This is not merely the *via negationis* (the negative way) of St. Thomas Aquinas, who (with the Cappadocians and all other true Christian theologians) insisted that this negative method is necessary to correct the manner of speaking in human concepts about God, which can never exhaust the infinite perfections found in Him. Such a theology attempts to speak of God by what He is not, rather than by what He *is*.

But the "father" of Christian mysticism, St. Gregory of Nyssa, opens theology up to the positive elements of the apophatic approach. He, along with his master, Origen, is one of the most original thinkers of the Eastern Church and the one who perhaps had the greatest influence in Christian mysticism. Pseudo-Dionysius in his treatise on *The Mystical Theology* is directly dependent upon Gregory. Through Pseudo-Dionysius this mysticism of darkness reached the West and influenced the Rhenish mystics of the 14th century: Meister Eckhart, Tauler and Suso, and the Flemish mystic, Jan Ruysbroeck. All of them had at least an indirect influence upon the Spanish mystics of the 16th century, chiefly St. John of the Cross and St. Teresa of Avila.

The theology of darkness is not original with Gregory but is basically derived from Philo (+44), the Alexandrian Hellenistic Jew. Both Gregory and Philo saw the mystical connotations of the Exodus theme as an analogy of the journey of the individual toward full union with God. It is especially in Gregory's treatise on *The Life of Moses* that we have a full presentation of the soul's journey up the mountain to meet God in the darkness of unknowing. In this work Gregory develops the meaning of darkness. Although it does mean (as has been already stated) that man possesses an incapacity to know God intimately, it primarily means that God is absolutely unfathomable, the fullness of being, and man can "understand" this only in darkness.

Such a dialectical, mystical apophatic theology holds that the "not" is the beginning of a knowledge of God by experience. It is based on the impossibility of defining God by human concepts, but not on the impossibility of somehow knowing Him. Such an approach is based, not on an absolute *no*, but on a relative *no*, a "pas encore," to quote Cyprian Kern.[6] There is a question of true, theological knowledge, but it is more in the experience of God as giving Himself to the repentant mystic who approaches God in a state of brokenness and interior poverty of spirit. Vladimir Lossky describes the knowledge of God beyond all conceptualization that St. Gregory of Nyssa called *theognosis*, knowledge taught by God:

> . . . *having failed to recognize the One it desires among the intelligible and incorporeal beings, and abandoning all that it finds, it recognizes the One it is seeking as the only One he does not comprehend. . . . Union with God is presented as a path which goes beyond vision and intelligence to the area where knowledge is suppressed and love alone remains —* or rather where *gnosis becomes* agape. [7]

We must note that the overwhelming infinity of God is nevertheless an experienced presence of God to the contemplative. But the modality of recognizing this presence is a new and higher form of knowledge that surpasses the powers and experiences of man. Thus St. Gregory resorts to such paradoxical terms as "luminous darkness," "sober inebriation," etc. He describes this *presence without seeing* in his *Commentary on the Song of Songs*:

> *The Bride is surrounded with the divine night in which the Bridegroom comes near without showing Himself . . . but by giving the soul a certain sense of His presence while fleeing from clear knowledge.* [8]

This is the positive, dialectical side to the apophatic theology of the Eastern Fathers. The Incomprehensible One is present and is experienced by the Christian. It is this very presence that is spoken of. It is that very transcendence that brings darkness to man's own reasoning powers. The emphasis is not on the incapacity of man, but rather on the overwhelming infinity of God that is nevertheless present.

Presence and transcendence are one in apophatic theology. In paradoxical fashion, the closer one gets to union with God the more blinding God becomes. This is not a matter of the knowledge of God becoming more abstruse but of the nature of God itself becoming more present. That presence brings to man the realization of the absolute awesomeness of the goal of his earthly journey.

Epectasis:
Love, Never Static, Always Growing

Gregory, who sought to rectify the teachings of Origen on the pre-existence of souls, nevertheless seized upon the truly positive insights of Origen and developed them further. A key insight taken from him is that the love of God in man is a force expanding his being and making him infinitely capable of possessing God in an unending process of greater growth. Gregory describes true perfection as "never to stop growing towards what is better and never to place any limit on perfection."[9]

Grace or the life of God within man, both in this life and in the life to come, presupposes growth in accepting a loving relationship with God and implies the necessity of constantly moving toward Him. Gregory writes: "Seeing that it is of the nature of Goodness to attract those who raise their eyes towards it, the soul keeps rising ever higher and higher."[10]

Gregory gives us two reasons, still viable for us today, why man's progress toward God can never come to an end. The first reason is that Beauty, God Himself, is infinite. The second reason is that the Beautiful is of such a nature that the desire for it can never be fully satisfied.[11] Gregory writes: "The soul that looks up toward God and conceives that good desire for His eternal beauty, constantly experiences an ever new yearning for that which lies ahead and her desire is never given its full satisfaction."[12]

God has implanted in every person, created "according to the Image and Likeness," the seed to be developed until — but then, it will never reach an *until*, according to Gregory. When can man

love God, the supreme Beauty enough? Can man ever say *enough*
to love when that love is God Himself? The soul ceases to mourn
when she discovers "that the true satisfaction of her desire consists
in constantly going on with her quest and never ceasing in her
ascent to God, seeing that every fulfillment of her desire continually generates a further desire for the Transcendent."[13]

St. Paul had written to the Philippians:

> *I can assure you my brothers, I am far from thinking that I
> have already won. All I can say is that I forget the past and I
> strain ahead for what is still to come; I am racing for the
> finish, for the prize to which God calls us upwards to receive
> in Christ Jesus (Ph 3:13-14).*

So, too, Gregory's mysticism is built upon *epectasis*, the
stretching out to possess the "Unpossessable." The Good, God as
Love, is limitless; our desire also must be limitless. In his *Life of
Moses*, Gregory states ". . . for it may be that human perfection
consists precisely in this constant growth in the good."[14]

For Gregory the unrest, the stretching forth to higher perfection, greater assimilation into the Absolute, the motion toward
greater being, is the same as stability.[15] Motion for Gregory
means more than moving from one stage of perfection to another.
The very transcendence of God is the reason that perfection itself is
constant motion. God is eternally at rest; yet He exists always in an
outgoing motion of love to share Himself with the other. Thus after
the mystic has been purified of all taint of self-absorption, God
attracts him continually to "keep rising ever higher and higher,
stretching with its desire for heavenly things to those that are before
(Ph 3:13), as the Apostle tells us, and thus it will always continue to
soar ever higher. . . . And thus the soul moves ceaselessly upwards,
always reviving its tension for its onward flight by means of the
progress it has already realized. Indeed, it is only spiritual activity
that nourishes its force by exercise; it does not slacken its tension by
action but rather increases it."[16]

Man's desire for God is insatiable. He reaches *hesychia*, tranquillity, as he purifies his desires and focuses them completely upon God. Yet this integration, this point of equilibrium, this stability is the beginning of motion towards greater perfection, the possession of God in greater consciousness It is the motion towards greater love and promise of greater life of the Bride in the Song of Songs: "On my bed, at night, I sought him, whom my heart loves. I sought but did not find him. So I will rise and go through the City; in the streets and the squares I will seek him whom my heart loves" (Sg 3:1-2).

Mystical Theology

It was, however, through the mysterious personage that history has called Dionysius the Areopagite, that these insights of St. Gregory of Nyssa would be handed down through the centuries in the famous, small treatise on *The Mystical Theology*.[17]   In this treatise, the apophatic approach reaches its peak in transforming theology into a contemplation of the mysteries of revelation. By allowing a real knowledge of God (but a higher one attainable by man as a divine gift) the Greek Fathers, whose doctrine Pseudo-Dionysius aptly summarizes, saw theology never as abstract, "working through concepts, but contemplative: raising the mind to those realities which pass all understanding. . . . It is not a question of suppressing the antinomy by adapting dogma to our understanding, but of a change of heart and mind enabling us to attain to the contemplation of the reality which reveals itself to us as it raises us to God, and unites us, according to our several capacities, to Him."[18]

In a classical passage, Pseudo-Dionysius describes the mystical side of true apophatic theology:

Nevertheless, he (Moses) did not attain to the Presence of God Himself; he saw not Him (for He cannot be looked

*upon), but the Place where He dwells. And this I take to
signify that the divinest and highest things seen by the eyes or
contemplated by the mind are but the symbolical expressions
of those that are immediately beneath Him who is above all.
Through these, His incomprehensible Presence is manifest
upon those heights of His Holy Places; that then it breaks
forth, even from that which is seen and that which sees, and
plunges the mystic into the Darkness of Unknowing, whence
all perfection of understanding is excluded, and he is en-
wrapped in that which is altogether intangible and
noumenal, being wholly absorbed in Him who is beyond all,
and in none else (whether himself or another); and through
the inactivity of all his reasoning powers is united by his
highest faculty to Him who is wholly unknowable; thus by
knowing nothing he knows that which is beyond his
knowledge.*[19]

A Living Theology

A correct apophatic theology is not opposed to cataphatic
theology. It encourages a positive theology expressed through
rational concepts, but it constantly tells positive theologians that
the expressions used by them are not really the way such and such a
perfection or relation exists in God. It stimulates them to open up to
the mystery of contact with the immanent God who comes in a
living experience.

The apparent conflicts between speculative and mystical
theology are resolved or made "livable" in the Liturgy of the
Church, the experiential drama of dogma that takes the faithful into
the heart of mystery to meet the living God of Abraham, Isaac and
Jacob beyond any concepts. The conflicts between a reasoned
theology and an apophatic mystical approach are resolved in the
living, liturgical prayer. "No language knows how to praise You

worthily and the mind, vaster than the world, becomes dizzy in celebrating You."[20]

Dogmatic, speculative theology can give us distinctions between substance and accidents and work out for us a theory of transubstantiation. It is, however, only in the immediate experience of celebrating the Eucharist and in receiving the Bread of Life that we come into a resolution of the antinomies of how eternity and time can meet, how Divinity can be joined with humanity, how Jesus Christ is both true God and true man eternally in glory and yet always coming into our lives to touch our human bodies with His glorious Body and Blood. Here we experience how we are Church, many members and yet each member uniquely loved by God, waiting for the full eschaton to come and yet in the Eucharist it has begun.

For one who has experienced the living theology so present in the Byzantine Holy Week and Easter Services, the reconciliation of cataphatic and apophatic theology is an experience that brings together antinomies and allows us to live in the power of such antinomies which function at the heart of our most transcendent, human experiences. On the vigil of Easter when the church is flooded with lighted candles and the priest sings out: "Christ is risen! He is truly risen!" one experiences the new victory of Christ over death. We find it easier to believe also that the same "divinizing process" has already begun in our lives and in those praying with us.

Not only do we believe it possible as when we recite the Nicene-Constantinople Creed each Sunday, but know it through experience, through a liturgical and ecclesiastical intuition. "The God-Man lies in sabbath repose and yet is risen. Creatures lament, the sun hides its rays, stars are lightless, but for us this Sabbath is blessed among all since Christ sleeps, to arise on the third day."[21]

Brokenness

Although we can intellectually understand something of God's presence in creation as loving energy, His real loving presence comes only in contemplative prayer. In this prayer we move beyond our own controlled activity to enter into God's healing love. But the first stage is for us to experience our own state of alienation from God. We must go inside of ourselves, into the deeper reaches of our consciousness and unconscious, beyond our controlled knowledge that can so easily lead us to illusions and greater separation from God, into those areas of brokenness, meaninglessness, death and darkness.

It is when we have the courage to confront our dark side that Jesus Christ becomes an energizing force of love as He releases His Spirit. We can then surrender to our loving Father who dwells within. He calls us evermore into our true nature as being one with His only begotten Son.

In the strange paradox of a living Christianity, the contemplative enters into darkness and desperately cries out for the light of Christ. Caught in the death of a static self-centeredness, the individual begins to sense the uncreated energies of God's new life ready to burst in upon him if he only stretches out to possess those energies.

Prayer is born in such inner poverty of spirit. Man learns in his existential nothingness that only God is life, is energy. All life must come from Him alone. He stretches out from his inner tomb for One to release him and bring him into new life. And in that yearning, he experiences a letting go of his own controlled existence as he knows his great need for the Other.

Call To Conversion

Scripture consistently reveals an intimate relationship between the divine persons as Trinity and human persons as individuals, created in the image and likeness of the community of God: the Father who is source and goal of all life; the Son in whose sonship we share; the Spirit as breath that sustains and sanctifies. This Spirit creates a passion in the heart of the individual person to stretch out and surrender to such inner Beauty. To accept God's invitation to enter into the divinizing process whereby we can really become children of God (1 Jn 3:1) is to respond to the call toward conversion.

Bernard Lonergan insists that what is basic in this *metanoia* (conversion) experience is the change of orientation. ". . . Religious conversion entails the adoption of a new orientation toward the absolutely Transcendent as self spoken within us and as spoken in the Word made flesh. . . ."[22] Such a conversion must transform our personhood and lifestyle. No one can see God's presence as love, inviting us to enter more fully into a reciprocal love relation with God and neighbor, without a subsequent and ongoing reconstruction of one's ideas, motivations and lifestyle.

Part of this conversion is to be able to know beyond the purely rational. It is the biblical "to know" which means "to enter into a personal relationship." In reality, the fullness of the human powers of reason, memory and affective will are involved in the conversion experience of revelation. It is an experienced call to go beyond (albeit through the human powers), to enter into a level of cosmic consciousness. On this level, God is experienced by our humanity in an "inter-penetration" through the Spirit of love and not solely through rational discourse.

God does not just "wait" for us to make up our minds. As His "lure," He pours His personalized love, the Holy Spirit, into His call to us. Our free response to this is made possible only by grace, because in His summons God gives what is asked. The potency of Jesus' consciousness of God as Father arouses in us the longing to be continually refashioned spiritually in the likeness of Jesus. This communication and the simultaneous gift of power is the person of

God's loving presence, His Holy Spirit. Man's spirit becomes one with God's Spirit (Rm 8:15).

Until the believer experiences such a metanoia, he/she is truly not yet a Christian, not yet converted to live in the consciousness of Jesus loving His Father. The Spirit desires to bring all persons to live the life of the Trinity, the primal community of an *I-Thou* in a *We* relationship. Conversion concerns our human lives in their entirety. Those "converted" in a never-ending process have the sober realization that their conversion is only the beginning of a daily fidelity to a lifetime of communion.

Children Of Freedom

We have pointed out some of the insights of the Eastern Christian Fathers who give us a corrective view to the over-emphasis of the rational approach that has often been the predominant view of Western Christianity. This "apophatic" theology has a positive emphasis on our human divinization into children of God by His energies of personalized self-giving to us in each moment of our human situation. It opens us up to experiential, direct and immediate knowledge of unifying love between the indwelling Trinity and the individual person. The Fathers hold out to us the fundamental message of the Gospel as God's continued call for us to be "converted," to be healed in His indwelling love. The Triune God gives us this love in His active energies of creative love.

Today we are searching for interior freedom in order to grow into our true selves. We hunger to be rid, both in ourselves and in society, of all the demonic forces that bind us to a darkening, crippling slavery. We wish to be freed of our sinful past, to grow unceasingly into fuller health and happiness. If we have deepened our awareness that God continually breathes into us His Spirit of love, we know that only the power of Jesus Christ can heal and free us to be what we should be by our first creation. Only He is the eternal Image of God the Father. We have been begotten in His

Spirit to be children of God and co-heirs with Him of Heaven forever.

True mysticism is the movement of a humble soul on fire with love for God towards greater union. In the growing assimilation into God's very life lies our consciousness of uniqueness. The mystic — who has experienced that God accepts, loves and suffers for him/her even to the point of accepting death on the cross — can alone love others as we should love. The mystic realizes that he/she has become fire and light. God, infinite love, loves within. Human wisdom is to be one with Him. This is love experienced that begets love towards others. True mysticism is authenticated by the love that the mystic shows towards others in humble service. This alone, the acceptance of others in self-sacrificing love, proves that the mystic has experienced a true love from the Source of all beauty and goodness. The mysticism that does not reap a harvest in shared love towards others is deceptive and dehumanizing. True mysticism is always begetting, becoming the other in greater unity of love. On this point, Eastern Christian mysticism has much to teach us.

A Relational God

We have seen how the Eastern Fathers complement and correct the heavily ''positive'' theology of the Western theologians through their apophatic, experiential approach to basic religious questions: How does God relate to us? Can we really experience Him directly, if He is so perfect and immutable in His nature?

Process theologians give their answer by positing the distinction between God's primal nature (which contains all possibilities before any creative relationships in time and space) and God's consequent nature (which is God cooperating with our human choices). By understressing the Trinity in order to emphasize a ''creating God,'' they also fail to stress the freedom of God always to be acting as a loving community in the context of our daily lives.

They lack the mystical sense of experiencing God directly through a higher knowledge, that of faith, hope and love given by the Holy Spirit when the individual is purified through asceticism and prayerful encounter with God in His uncreated energies of love. Let us now turn to the teaching of the Eastern Christian Fathers on God's energies in order to keep together in tension the paradox that God is infinitely transcendent and independent of us in His essence or divine nature, and yet as a loving Triune community is always outpouring Himself in creative, energetic actions.

ENDNOTES

1 Thomas Merton gives this detail of Barth's life in *Conjectures of a Guilty Bystander* (Garden City: Doubleday, 1966), p. 3.

2 Henri Bergson: *The Two Sources of Morality and Religion*; tr. by R. Ashley Audra & Cloudesley Brereton (N.Y.: Henry Holt & Co., 1935), p. 257.

3 R. Otto: *The Idea of the Holy*; tr. by J.W. Harvey (N.Y.: Oxford Univ. Press, 1958), pp. 8-10.

4 Evagrius: *On Prayer* in: *Early Fathers from the Philokalia*; tr. by E. Kadloubovsky & G. Palmer (London: Faber & Faber, 1954), no. 54, p. 133.

5 St. John Damascene: *De Fide Orthodoxa*; Bk. 50; 4: *PG* 94, 800 B.

6 Cyprian Kern: "Les elements de la théologie de Grégorie Palamas," in: *Irénikon*, 20 (1947), p. 9.

7 Vladimir Lossky: *Vision of God* (Clayton, WI: Faith Press, 1963), pp. 71, 74.

8 St. Gregory of Nyssa: *Commentary on the Song of Songs*; *PG* 44, 1001B.

9 St. Gregory of Nyssa: *On Perfection*; tr. by Virginia Woods Callahan in: *Ascetical Works of Gregory of Nyssa* (*Fathers of the Church*, Vol. 58) (Washington, DC: Catholic Univ. Press, 1967), p. 122.

10 St. Gregory of Nyssa: *The Life of Moses*, cited in: *From Glory to Glory*; ed. by J. Danielou and H. Musurillo (N.Y.: Scribner, 1961), p. 144.

11 Ibid., p. 148.

12 *Commentary on the Song of Songs*; cited in: *From Glory to Glory*, p. 270.

13 Ibid.

14 *The Life of Moses*: *PG* 44; 301C; cited in: *From Glory to Glory*, p. 83.

15 Ibid., p. 149.

16 Ibid., p. 144.

17 Pseudo-Dionysius: *The Mystical Theology*, in: *Mysticism: A Study and Anthology*; ed. by F.C. Happold (Baltimore: Penguin, 1971), pp. 215-216.

18 Cited by V. Lossky: *The Mystical Theology of the Eastern Church* (London: James Clarke & Co., 1957), p. 43.

19 Pseudo-Dionysius: *Mystical Theology*, p. 214.

20 The feast of the Epiphany; Matins, Canon 9, of the Byzantine Rite.

21 Holy Saturday Matins of the Byzantine Rite.

22 Bernard Butler: "Bernard Lonergan and Conversion," in: *Worship*, 49 (June), p. 330.

CHAPTER

5

God's Creative Energies

An inscription carved over the doorway of Dr. Carl Jung's house in Kusnacht/Zurich reads in Latin: "Vocatus Atque non Vocatus, Deus Aderit" ("Called and not called, God will be there"). True Christianity struggles always to present God both as unapproachable in His awesome majesty and perfect essence, and as pursuing us in our brokenness. We have presented the ideas of the Eastern Christian Fathers concerning their apophatic theology. They maintain in happy tension the awesome transcendence of an infinitely perfect God and the immanence of a Triune, loving community which seeks to divinize us through their indwelling presence. Our very brokenness and inner poverty of spirit prepare us for such a mystical oneness with God Himself.

The Unapproachable One

In such brokenness, the Christian knows that God is unreachable and unknowable. No matter how poor and empty we know ourselves to be, we do begin to feel God's infilling come upon us. God is always truly there! Still, we also know that we will never in this earthly existence see Him face to face. Yahweh shows Himself to us as He did to Moses; it is only His "back" that we see. "Then I will take my hand away and you shall see the back of me; but my face is not to be seen" (Ex 33:23).

None of us can ever see God fully. "No one has ever seen God" (1 Jn 4:12; Jn 1:18; 6:46). We would need to be God, part of His essence, in order to know Him fully. Only a like nature could comprehend His nature. In spite of the revelation of the Father's love made to us by His Son, Jesus Christ, we shall never know Him fully. No matter how inflamed with His loving presence we have become, both in this life and in the life to come, there will always be something *unfathomable* about God.

And that is why the Greek Fathers always insisted on the distinction between God's *essence* and His uncreated *energies*. This distinction is of paramount importance. On the one hand, it preserves the awesome transcendence of God that can never be totally possessed by finite creatures. In God's essence He is immutable, all perfect, unchanging. We in no way can add anything to His perfections. God is completely independent of us.

Still, we know from God's revelation in Scripture that in His holiness and humility He wishes to share His life with us. If God is love (1 Jn 4:8), He must "go forth" out of Himself to be present to another, to share His being with that other. Thus God creates the whole world in order that He may share Himself through His gifts with us. Only we stand amidst all creatures as the ones made in God's image and likeness (Gn 1:26).

Only we possess an *unfinished* nature that has been gifted by God with spiritual faculties to communicate with His knowledge and love. We can freely receive God's communications and answer His call to become *divinized*, to be elevated into sharing by *participation* in God's very nature (2 P 1:4). The aim for which God has created us is that we might enter into a living union in knowledge and love with Him and in Him to find our complete happiness.

Deification

Thus the early Fathers saw our fulfilled human nature as one in Jesus Christ. He is the image of the invisible God (Col 1:15) and we have been made in and through that image (Jn 1:3). "God's love for us was revealed when God sent into the world his only Son so that we could have life through him" (1 Jn 4:9). The redeeming work of the crucified and risen Jesus consists in giving us His Spirit of love through whom we may know the Father and the fullness of the Son (Jn 17:3) and thus we ourselves can become truly children of God (Jn 1:12; Rm 8:15; Gal 4:6).

This "going-forth" of God, to use Pseudo-Dionysius' term, is simply *grace* in the primal sense. It is God in His *hesed* covenantal love, pursuing His people as He stretches out His "two Hands — Jesus Christ and the Holy Spirit", as St. Irenaeus in the second century was fond of saying.

All of God's creative, loving energies are focused upon the mystery of God's free choice of us to become His holy people in Christ Jesus:

Before the world was made, he chose us,
chose us in Christ,
to be holy and spotless, and to live through love in his
    presence,
determining that we should become his
adopted sons, through Jesus Christ
for his own kind purposes,
to make us praise the glory of his grace,
his free gift to us in the Beloved,
in whom, through his blood, we gain our
freedom, the forgiveness of our sins (Ep 1:4-7).

God, therefore, is *grace* as He goes out of Himself in His uncreated energies to share His very own life with us. We can, then, truly know God and experience Him. Although in His

Godhead He is totally incomprehensible, He can be experienced in His energies. The Good News consists of God's revelation of Himself as a loving Father, giving Himself to us through His Son Jesus in His Spirit. In experiencing this, we can know God in His love toward us. And we can cooperate with God's loving energies to be loving energies toward others. If we cannot first "experience" God's love for us (which is the essence of *contemplation*), we will never be able to give true, self-sacrificing love to others. And without genuine love we die!

Dwelling In The Trinity

In the famous text of 2 Peter 1:4, "through these promises you may become partakers of the divine nature," we are given a solid biblical basis for this union between God and man — God dwelling in us and we in Him. This is a constant theme in St. John's Gospel and also in the Epistles of St. Paul, who sees the Christian life above all else as a life "in Christ."[1]

Behind this doctrine there lies the idea of man made according to the "image and likeness" of God, the Holy Trinity. Just as the three Persons of the Trinity "dwell" in one another in an unceasing movement of love, so we, made in their image, are called to dwell in the Triune God. "May they all be one," Christ prayed at the Last Supper, "as you are in me and I in you, so also may they be one in us" (Jn 17:21).

Christ prays that we may share in the life of the Trinity, in a movement of love which passes between the divine Persons. He prays that we may be taken up into the Godhead — a personal and organic union between God and man.[2]

According to the 4th century mystic, Evagrius, to know the mystery of the Trinity in its fullness is to enter into perfect union with God and to attain to the deification of the human creature. In other words, it is to enter into the very life of the Holy Trinity and to become in St. Peter's words, "partakers of the divine nature."[3]

The revelation of God the Holy Trinity — Father, Son and Holy Spirit — is, in fact, the basis of all Christian theology. In the sense in which the word was understood by the Greek Fathers, it is theology itself which stands for the mystery of the Trinity revealed to the Church.[4]

Trinitarian theology is a theology of union, a mystical theology which appeals to experience. It presupposes a continuous and progressive series of changes in created nature, a more and more intimate communion of the human person with the Holy Trinity.

Importance Of Essence-Energy Distinction

Hereafter, the idea of deification must always be understood in the light of the distinction between God's essence and His energies. Union with God means union with the divine energies, not with His divine essence.

Another extremely important point is that in this mystical union, Creator and creature do not become fused into a single being that swallows us up in the deity. The Eastern Church insists that we, however closely linked to God, retain our full personal integrity. We, when deified, remain distinct (though not separate) from God. Nor do we cease to be human. We remain creatures while "becoming god by grace," as Christ remained God when becoming man by the Incarnation. The Orthodox historian Timothy Ware insists that man does not become god by nature, but is merely a "created god," a god by grace.[5]

What, then, is the nature of the relationship by which we are able to enter into union with the Holy Trinity? If we were able to be united to the very essence of God and to participate in it in the very least degree, we should not be what we are. We should be god by nature. God, then, would no longer be Trinity, but myriads of hypostases (self-existing persons), for He would have as many hypostases as there would be persons participating in His essence. God, therefore, is and remains inaccessible to us in His essence.[6]

Can we say, then, that it is with one of the Three Divine Persons that we enter into union? This would be the hypostatic union proper to the Son alone, in whom God becomes man without ceasing to be the Second Person of the Trinity. Even though we share the same human nature as Christ and receive in Him the name of children of God. we do not ourselves become the divine hypostasis or person of the Son by the fact of the Incarnation. We are unable, therefore, to participate in either the essence or the hypostases of the Holy Trinity. We are compelled to recognize in God an ineffable distinction (other than that between His essence and His Persons) according to which He is, under different aspects, both totally inaccessible and at the same time accessible. This distinction is between   (1) the essence or nature of God, which is inaccessible, unknowable and incommunicable, and   (2) the energies or divine operations, in which He goes forth from Himself, manifests, communicates and gives Himself. Vladimir Lossky, a 20th century Russian theologian, writes: "The divine and deifying illumination and grace is not the essence but the energy of God, a divine power and energy common to the nature in three. Thus, according to St. Gregory Palamas of the 14th century, 'to say that the divine nature is communicable not in itself, but through its energy, is to remain within the bounds of right devotion.' "[7]

Patristic Teaching

This theology, although explicated in the 14th century by St. Gregory Palamas, is not new. It was taught centuries earlier. St. Basil, for example, talks of the role of the energies: "It is by His energies that we say we know our God; we do not assert that we can come near to the essence itself, for His energies descend to us, but His essence remains unapproachable."[8]

St. Maximus the Confessor expresses the same idea when he says: "God is communicable in what He imparts to us; but He is not communicable in the incommunicability of His essence."[9]   The

Fathers call the energies "rays of divinity," penetrating the created universe. Gregory Palamas calls them simply "divinities," or "uncreated light" or "grace."

The favorite image of the sun emitting its rays to the earth is used by St. Gregory of Nyssa and would be repeated by all the succeeding Eastern Christian theologians, especially by St. Gregory Palamas. St. Gregory of Nyssa writes:

> As the sun, according to the divine dispensation, temperating the vigor and sincerity of its rays by the intermediate air, emits to those receiving it a proportionate splendor and heat, remaining by itself unapproachable to the weakness of our nature, thus also the divine power, by a similarity to the given example, infinitely surpassing our nature and inaccessible to participation . . . gives to the human nature what is in her power to receive.[10]

The doctrine concerning the energies is not a mere abstract conception, or an intellectual distinction. We are dealing with a strictly concrete reality of a revealed truth of Christianity.

A Christian Realism

God's presence in His energies must be understood in a realistic way. It is not the presence of a cause operative in its effects, for the energies are not effects of the divine cause, as creatures are. They are not created, but flow eternally from the one essence of the Trinity. They are the outpourings of the divine nature which cannot set bounds to itself, for God is more than essence. God exists both in His essence and outside of His essence. Gregory Palamas puts it this way: "Creation is the task of energy; it is for nature to beget."[11]

If the real distinction between essence and energies is denied, we could not fix any clear borderline between the procession of the divine persons and the creation of the world: both would be equal acts of the divine nature and the being and the action of God would be the same. It becomes necessary, therefore, to distinguish in God His nature, which is one, and three hypostases, and the uncreated energies which proceed forth from the nature. If we participate in God in His energies, according to our own capacity, this does not contradict the fact that God manifests Himself fully in His procession. He is wholly present in each ray of His divinity.[12]

The manifestation of the Trinity toward us creatures may be seen as the Father operating by the Son in the Holy Spirit. The work of creation is common to the whole Trinity, but each of the three Persons is the cause of created being in a way which is different from the other two Persons, though in each case all three are united to each other.

In regard to the divine energies, there are two possibilities of error to be avoided.

The first is that energy is not a divine function which exists on account of creatures, despite the fact that it is through His energies, which penetrate everything that exists, that God creates and operates. Even if creatures did not exist, God would manifest Himself beyond His essence, just as the sun would shine whether or not there were any beings capable of receiving its light.

Secondly, the created world does not become infinite and coeternal with God because the natural processions or divine energies are so. The existence of the energies implies no necessity in the act of creation, which is freely effected by the divine energy but determined by a decision of the common will of the three persons. Creation is an act of the will of God which makes a new subject come into being outside the divine being, through God's free manifestation.

It is in creatures — beings created from nothing by the divine will, limited and subject to change — that the infinite and eternal energies abide, making the greatness of God to shine forth in all things, and appearing beyond all things as the divine light which the created world cannot contain.

The Mystical Life

Summing up the Eastern Church's position in regard to un-created energy, three distinctions are of great importance in the concept of the mystical life.

1. The doctrine of the energies ineffably distinct from the essence, is the dogmatic basis of the real character of all mystical experience. God, who is inaccessible in His essence, is present in His energies "as in a mirror, remaining invisible in that which He is: in the same way we are able to see our faces, themselves invisible to us, in a glass," in the words of St. Gregory Palamas.

2. This doctrine makes it possible to understand how the Trinity can remain incommunicable in essence and at the same time come and dwell within us, according to the promise of Christ. The presence is not a causal one, such as in creation. Neither is it a presence according to the essence which is by definition incom-municable. It is a mode according to which the Trinity dwells in us by means of grace — for it is by this name that we know the deifying energies which the Holy Spirit communicates to us.

3. The distinction between the essence and energies allows us to unite with God in His energies, or by grace, making us partici-pate in the divine nature, without our essence becoming thereby the essence of God.

These antinomial or seemingly paradoxical distinctions are set forth to safeguard the mystery while yet expressing the data of revealed dogma. Thus, in the doctrine of the Trinity, the distinction between the Persons and nature revealed a tendency to represent God as a "monad and triad in one" with the consequence that the domination of the unity of nature over the trinity of the hypostases was avoided, as was the danger of minimizing the primordial mystery of the identity-diversity. In the same way, the distinction between the essence and the energies is due to the antinomy between the unknowable and the knowable, the incommunicable and the communicable, with which both religious thought and experience of divine things are ultimately faced. These real distinctions introduce no "composition" into the divine being. They signify the mystery of God, who is absolutely one according to His nature, absolutely three according to His Persons, sovereign and inaccessible Trinity, dwelling in the profusion of glory which is His uncreated light, His eternal kingdom into which all must enter who inherit the deified state.

The Nature Of God's Energies

God's energies, therefore, are really God in His loving relationships toward us. God's activities can never be divided into those that are *sacred* and those that are merely *secular*, between those that are *natural* and those that are *supernatural*. The energies are God, who in His essence is unapproachable and simple, yet who in His condescending love is *always* (hence *uncreated*) manifesting Himself to us in diverse ways. They are God's showing Himself in self-giving to us human beings.

Archbishop Joseph Raya gives us a beautiful description of God's energies that summarizes well the Greek patristic teaching:

> *It is not God's action but God himself in his action who makes himself known to man and gives him the ability to "see" him. God enters into man's love, remaining there in his intimate reality. This presence is real, indeed most real. This communication of God himself is called, "Uncreated Energy." The uncreated energies of God are not 'things' which exist outside of God, not 'gifts' of God; they are God himself in his action. They are the very God who is himself Uncreated. They are therefore called 'uncreated' because their cause and origin is the Essence of God. In them God, as it were, goes beyond himself and becomes 'transradiant' in order to really communicate himself. Thus the Essence and energies of God are not 'parts' of God but two ways by which we human beings can contemplate God's essence.*[13]

In such a biblical and patristic vision *grace* is not primarily a "thing" that God places upon our nature to give us "something" extrinsic in order to perfect our being. Grace is, first of all, God's presence as activating love. His love is always present, permeating us, surrounding us, drawing us in all things by His love into greater oneness with Him. The energies are God in loving and creative relationships to share His holiness and inner life with us. They are not the *created* relationships that result from God's loving activities; they are truly *God-in-action* for us.

We find a description in the Book of Habakkuk of God's energies:

> *Eloah is coming from Teman,*
> *and the Holy One from Mount Paran.*
> *His majesty veils the heavens,*
> *the earth is filled with his glory.*
> *his brightness is like the day,*
> *rays flash from his hands,*
> *that is where his power lies hidden (Hab 3:3-4).*

Yahweh is an omnipresent God who by His creative Word fills all creatures and brings them into being (Ps 33:6-9). Where can we ever escape from God's Spirit (Ps 139:7)? The prophet Jeremiah presents a God who fills all things:

> *Can anyone hide in a dark corner*
> *without my seeing him? — It is Yahweh who speaks,*
> *Do I not fill*
> *heaven and earth? — it is Yahweh who speaks (Jr 23:24).*

Loving Energies

The energies of God flow out from the three Persons within the Trinity. They are real (although not material nor merely an intellectual concept). They are essential, i.e. not an accident; they flow truly from the essence of the Godhead. Yet they are distinct from the actual essence of the Godhead.[14]   These energies are essentially personified. They are the whole Trinity acting in loving relationships toward all creatures.

In such a vision we can readily see that for the Greek Fathers God can never be static in His activities toward us and His creation. Because the energies are personalized, they are a common manifestation of the Persons of the Trinity. If God's energies were not personalized, we would not truly share in God's own life through His self-giving. We would not be truly regenerated. Grace, then, would be a thing God heaps upon us, a thing different from His own being. Man would be divinized only in an extrinsic way and not by direct contact with God's own life.

Nor are we divinized in a Hindu or Buddhist fashion of non-duality (*Advaita*) where we would be assimilated into the Godhead while losing any human uniqueness, as a drop of water flows into the ocean.

A Conversion Experience

God is, therefore, permeating all persons, all things, all events by His personalized, loving, uncreated energies. Everything is "graced" by God at each moment. It is for the human person, the contemplative, to have new eyes to see the loving presence of God in His Trinitarian energies in all creatures, in every event.

G.M. Hopkins beautifully captures this presence of God in nature and the need on our part to "behold" that energizing, loving presence:

> *And the azurous hung hills are his world-wielding shoulder*
> *Majestic — as a stallion stalwart, very-violent-sweet!*
> *These things, these things were here and but the beholder*
> *Wanting; which two when they once meet,*

The heart rears wings bold and bolder
 And hurls for him, O half hurls earth for him off his
feet.[15]

Such a contemplative "sees" God progressively more and more in all creatures and in all events. But it is only through a purification process that the Greek Fathers call *praxis* that one can see the energies of God bathe the whole universe and charge it with His infinite love.

It is what Teilhard de Chardin calls "passionate indifference." It is a passionate seeking of the loving Father's face in each event and a total detachment from one's own impetuous control over such an event. Such a mental balance, an interiorly disciplined control to bring all moods and feelings under God's dominion, is what St. Paul describes: "Every thought is our prisoner, captured to be brought into obedience to Christ" (2 Cor 10:5).

It is a constant living in faith that strips the covering away from the experience of the moment to reveal God's loving, dynamic, energetic presence at the heart of matter. Through such faith and a child-like trust in God, the Christian surrenders to God's love, present in every place, in each event at each moment.

A Continual Growth

We begin to see the importance of the asceticism of our daily lives, often so full of banality, monotony, boredom, even seemingly a dull meaninglessness. There are also positive, self-fulfilling moments in our daily work, our human relationships, our moments of recreation. But it is in such a daily context that we are to discover God pouring Himself out to us by His divine energies — always that He might share with us His own life and happiness.

It is easy to see, therefore, that the very nature of grace as God's life within us presupposes growth. When have we received enough of God's own life? When have we exhausted our discern-

ment of God's presence in each new event? Each moment brings
the exciting possibility of new growth, dependent upon our surrender to God's loving activity in each event. To accept God's
loving presence *now* means to become more open to it in the next
moment.

St. Gregory of Nyssa writes: "The grace of the Holy Spirit is
given to everyone with the understanding that there is to be an
augmenting and increase of what is received."[16]

Bodily Integration

God is present in all things with His loving activity. It follows
that, as we enter into a spiritual, *faithful* contemplation of His
energizing presence everywhere, we should see God working in
our very own bodies to bring them into a harmony of "spirit, soul
and body" (1 Th 5:23). The Bible contrasts the man of the flesh
(*sarx*) — i.e., one living only for himself, not *in* Christ — and the
Christian graced by the Holy Spirit. "Material" and "immaterial"
as a Platonic dichotomy of opposites are not found in Holy
Scripture.

As we open totally to God on all levels of spirit, soul and body
relationships, God's "graceful" energies elevate us into an integration as His children. Jesus was the most integrated human
being who ever lived because He found His Heavenly Father
working in loving activity in all such relationships. He discovered
the Father loving Him in His spirit *and* in His body. Jesus could
enjoy the Father's love in *being* there, in His body. His body was
also the *place* where the Father's energies were at work.

Jesus, therefore, used His body as a gift to communicate
God's Spirit in love to all whom He met. If St. Paul could write to
his fellow Christians: "Your body, you know, is the temple of the
Holy Spirit" (1 Cor 6:19), how much more must have Jesus known
the sacredness of His body? The whole man Jesus was the Son of
God.

Thus we also are to be whole persons, ever growing into a greater likeness to Christ by grace, by God's uncreated energies. Such a holistic approach, as taught by the Greek Fathers, is summarized by St. Gregory Palamas:

> The spiritual joy that comes from the spirit into the body is not at all broken by communion with the body, but transforms the body and makes it spiritual, for then it rejects all the evil appetites of the flesh, and does not drag the body down any more but rises up with it so that the whole man becomes "Spirit" according to what is written: "He who is born of the Spirit is Spirit" (Jn 3:6, 8).[17]

This is an important conclusion to the truth that, if God's energies touch us in our bodily relationships, then the body can experience the effects of God's loving activities. Our Platonic or Jansenistic concept of the body as something basically evil, or at least not very sacred, must change to a more incarnational view. Such a view should encourage us in the way we feed and clothe our bodies, in the way we find God in our sexuality, even in the way we can use the body to pray to God.

Diaphanous Matter

A spirituality that "sees" God working in the material world through His loving energies has great repercussions for our daily living. If God is ever present and acting in the material world by His energies, can we speak of a distinction between the sacred and the profane? Can any creature in itself be objectively "profane"? Does not the term "secular" apply to a person who fails to see God "inside" of matter? Is not the whole world sacred for the contemplative who sees God shining through that world in a diaphany?

For such contemplatives in touch with the reality of God present everywhere in His loving energies, the world is never merely "natural," waiting for God to add His "supernatural" grace. "The world is charged with the grandeur of God. It will flame out, like shining from shook foil."[18]

Gerard Manley Hopkins once wrote a fitting description of God's uncreated energies. "All things are charged with love, are charged with God and if we know how to touch them, give off sparks and take fire, yield drops and flow, ring and tell of him."

God's creative presence shines like a light to such contemplatives. They see how each creature tumbles forth continually through God's own personal, loving involvement. They do not seek to exploit or conquer nature, but rather — in an attitude of ever-increasing receptivity — they seek to discover God in all things, and all things in God. They wish to serve Him and to render Him more adored and glorified throughout the entire universe.

A Gift From God

To see God in all His omnipresent, creative presence and to love and adore Him in all His works is a gift of contemplation given us by God. Teilhard de Chardin well describes this intuitive grasp of God as a seeing and a taste, but above all as a gift:

> The perception of the divine omnipresence is essentially a seeing, a taste, that is to say, a sort of intuition bearing upon certain superior qualities in things. It cannot, therefore, be attained directly by any process of reasoning, nor by any human artifice. It is a gift, like life itself, of which it is undoubtedly the supreme experimental perfection. . . . To experience the attraction of God, to be sensible of the beauty, the consistency and the final unity of being, is the highest and at the same time the most complete of our 'passivities of growth.' God tends, by the logic of His creative effort, to make Himself sought and perceived by us. . . . His prevenient grace is therefore always on the alert to

*excite our first look and our first prayer. But in the end the
initiative, the awakening, always come from Him, and whatever the further developments of our mystical faculties, no
progress is achieved in this domain except as the new response to a new gift.* [19]

Through such a gift of contemplation, God allows us to move
through His world with a childlike spirit of wonderment. God is
everywhere present! We pierce through the ordinary, the prosaic,
even the brokenness and sordidness of this world to "unveil" the
loving presence of God inside of matter. A worshipful reverence, a
taste for the sublime comes over us in the most casual events
because the Spirit of God speaks to us in "the silent allusion of
things to a meaning greater than themselves," as Abraham J.
Heschel writes. [20]

Love For Others

God's greatest display of uncreated energies is found in His
loving presence within human friendships. Here God's Spirit
reaches the fullness of the creative process as He works to bring
two or more gathered together in Christ's name (Mt 18:20) into a
greater oneness in the Body of Christ. Paradoxically, the Spirit also
creates, besides the experience of multiplicity in unity, the profound sense of the uniqueness of each person loving and being
loved.

"God is love and anyone who lives in love lives in God and
God lives in him" (1 Jn 4:16). The more deeply we move in loving
relationships towards others, the more deeply we experience God's
activating love within us. The peak of true contemplation of God's
loving energies is to experience them as the moving force in our
free surrender in tender, loving care for others.

As we consciously seek to yield to God's loving presence in
each human encounter, we are swept up into the heart of God's own

love, being poured out in a fresh release through our free cooperation. It is truly God's own life and love as one energy force within
us, empowering us with a transforming love to release that same
uncreated energy of love potentially stored up in the heart of each
person we meet.

Love's Paradox

Thus we come to the great paradox of the mystery of God's
love as uncreated energies. God's love is uncreated, always
present, always loving. Yet these great energies of God's love for
His children cannot be discovered and released except through His
loving children. God, so powerful, so independent and transcendent over all His creatures, has humbly tied Himself and the
manifestation of His love to us human beings.

We are truly called to be "reconcilers" of the whole world, as
St. Paul speaks of those who are "in Christ Jesus" (2 Cor 5:18).
God is uniting the multiplied world into the Body of Christ through
His uncreated energies experienced in prayer as the personal love
that He has for the individual. God becomes energized,
personalized love for His world as we become signs of the new
creation by those very energies of love experienced within our
loves.

As we allow those energies to shine forth from our lives into
the lives of others through the love we have towards them, God
becomes Love manifested in His world.

If we have experienced grace as God's personal, loving
presence within ourselves we are impelled by God's energies of
love to be oriented outwardly towards others. Heaven is no longer a
place to go to after death. It is a process of yielding to the inner,
transforming power of God's love, living with n all who are in
Christ Jesus. Such transfigured Christians go into the world, not
only to bring the creative energies of God, but also to "unconceal"
His loving energies already present in His world.

Human Energies Of love

These Christians do not wait for a Heaven to come. In loving responsibility to God, they release His loving energies within the human scene that — by God's providence — they are privileged in time and space to be a part of. As Thomas Merton says, "It is only in assuming full responsibility for our world, for our lives and for ourselves that we can be said to live really for God."[21]

God as uncreated energies of love is always calling us to be a loving energy in our world. Heaven is already this wonderful world, as seen by faith, hope and love, as bathed in God's transfiguring power of love. But it is also a return to loving energy on our part to cooperate with God's love to bring this world into the Body of Christ. This is true contemplation. It begins in experiencing God's energies of love transforming us in prayer, alone with God, into loved children of the Heavenly Father. It continues as a movement outward into the material world where we contemplate God's loving presence in an active surrender of ourselves to be His energizing love toward all whom we meet. God's uncreated energies ultimately are manifested in loving, humble service to each other. Only this can release the energies of God's presence in our world so that they can fulfill (with human cooperation) God's eternal plan to bring all things into a oneness with Christ. ". . . because God wanted all perfection to be found in him and all things to be reconciled through him and for him" (Col 1:19-20).

ENDNOTES

1 Timothy Ware: *The Orthodox Church* (Baltimore, MD: Penguin, 1972), p. 236.
2 Ibid., p. 238.
3 Vladimir Lossky: *The Mystical Theology of the Eastern Church* (London: James Clarke & Co., 1968), p. 67.
4 Ibid.
5 Ware, pp. 236-242.
6 Lossky, pp. 68-69.
7 Ibid., p. 70.

8 St. Basil: *Epistle to Amphilochius*; cited by G. Habra: "The Patristic Sources of the Doctrine of Gregory Palamas on the Divine Energies," in: *Eastern Churches Quarterly*; 12 (1957-1958), p. 300.

9 Cited by Lossky, p. 73.

10 St. Gregory of Nyssa: *Against Eunomius*, XII, cited by G. Habra, p. 300.

11 Cited by Lossky, p. 74.

12 Ibid., p. 76.

13 Archbishop Joseph Raya: *The Face of God* (Denville, NJ: Dimension Books, 1976), pp. 37-38.

14 Cf. my work: *A Theology of Uncreated Energies* (Milwaukee: Marquette Univ. Press, 1978), Ch. 3, pp. 60-98.

15 Gerard Manley Hopkins, S.J.: "Hurrahing in Harvest," in *A Hopkins Reader*; ed. by John Peck (N.Y. & London: Oxford Univ. Press, 1953), p. 15.

16 St. Gregory of Nyssa: *The Christian Mode of Life*, in: *The Fathers of the Church* (Washington, D.C., 1967), Vol. 58, p. 130.

17 *Grégorie Palamas: Les Triads pour la defense des Saints Hesychastes*; 3 vols., ed. by John Meyendorff (Louvain: Spicilegium Sacrum Lovaniense, 1959); Triads II, 2.9.

18 G.M. Hopkins: "God's Grandeur," in *A Hopkins Reader*, p. 13.

19 Pierre Teilhard de Chardin: *The Divine Milieu* (N.Y.: Harper & Bros., 1960), p. 111.

20 A.J. Heschel: *God in Search of Man* (N.Y.: Farrar, Straus & Giroux, 1955), p. 39.

21 Thomas Merton: *Contemplation in a World of Action* (Garden City, N.Y.: Doubleday, 1971), p. 54.

The Cosmic Christ

The Eastern Fathers have led us to the "within" of matter. There in humility and reverence for God's "numinous" transcendence, they show us — through their teachings on God's uncreated energies of love — how to discover the immanent presence of God in the process of co-creating with us the world of diversity into unity through love.

Yet their teachings, based on God's revelation through Scripture and their own mystical experiences, are seemingly inadequate to convince us moderns today. They could not have had the knowledge we possess through science of our universe as one of gigantic proportions, of staggering energies and masses, of chaotic upheavals with great potentiality for destruction as well as creativity.

Their world view had all things created directly by God. Their theology gave a simple picture of the purpose and direction of the cosmos. Modern scientific discoveries unfold to us a world of tremendous energies on all macrocosmic and microcosmic levels. The apparent "faith" view of the early Fathers does not help us cope with the great paradox of the coexistence of apparent order and purpose with chaos and purposelessness. We struggle with order and disorder, with necessity and change, in a world that is expanding through an exploding process of evolution.

Can we not attribute in some degree the growing secularization of our modern world and its pathetic search for transcendence to our separation of two ways of knowing? Scientists give us a knowledge of the universe in all its complexities as they probe back in time to the origin of the universe in the "big bang." They split the atom and tell us of the minute complexity of the subatomic particles. Yet scientists in their discovered world of chance, randomness and chaos cannot tell us where the world process is going and whether a synthesis of order and harmony will ever result at the end of the struggle.

A Universe Without A Theology

Teilhard de Chardin, the French Jesuit and paleontologist, who died in 1955, faced this separation of two worlds of knowledge when he wrote:

> In the space of two or three centuries, and under the converging influence of a number of factors . . . it has become impossible to present the universe to us in the form of an established harmony: we now see unmistakably that it is a system in movement. It is no longer an order but a process. No longer a cosmos but a cosmogenesis.[1]

Let us turn in this chapter to the ideas of Pierre Teilhard de Chardin[2] in order to discover God at the heart of matter. He can teach us a theology of the universe through his model of the cosmic Christ, a theology that finds its basic faith vision in the writings of St. Paul, St. John and the early Fathers of the Christian East. We can learn to love the universe of matter and find God through Christ, immanently present in each atom and directing all (with our human, free cooperation) in love into greater complexities of diversity in unity through creative action.

Teilhard articulates the dilemma of the modern believer. On the one hand he asks: "Will the material world remain ever closed to modern man in his attempt to find God? Will man yield himself to the material world, whose many mysteries he does not understand, as though it were uncontrollable, and hence incomprehensible to the human mind? Or will he merely abandon the material world and the possibility of ever rising through it to find God in the very heart of matter?"

On the other hand modern man's religious problem concerns the fundamental questions of faith, God and Christ. Does the historical Christ have any real relevance for the modern Christian? Can the Christ of the Gospels be found in the universe that science unfolds to us? Teilhard sensed this growing restlessness as early as 1927 when he wrote the most complete synthesis of his spiritual vision, *The Divine Milieu*, for those who were asking, "Is the Christ of the Gospels, imagined and loved within the dimensions of a Mediterranean world, capable of still embracing and still forming the center of our prodigiously expanded universe? Is the world not in the process of becoming more vast, more close, more dazzling than Jehovah? Will it not burst our religion asunder? Eclipse our God?"[3]

Jesus Christ, in a theology of "up there," seems too remote for the modern man thirsting for a personal encounter with the God he so ardently wants to love, not merely on Sundays, but every moment of his life. The devotion to Christ the King popularized by St. Bernard of Clairvaux and St. Ignatius of Loyola in an age of feudal chivalry, contemplated Christ as the perfect model, the divine example of human goodness. A Christian was to reconstruct in his mind the life of our Lord, mull over His example and words, and then strive to imitate the divine model by thinking and acting in a Christ-like manner.

Today's psychology of personal encounter stresses that the knowledge of another person leading to a person-to-person relationship in love is not merely conceptual. The question is not an essential one of "what he is" but an existential one of "who he is" who is being encountered. The individuality, that which makes this person uniquely *this* person, can never be captured completely in a mental concept.

The inner core of a person remains sealed off to others unless a mutual love engenders a deeper insight into *who* this person is. In our encounter with Christ today it is not enough to contemplate Him as the historical person revealed in the Gospels. Nor is it enough to contemplate Him in the encounter of faith through grace by which we become united with Him and the other members of His Mystical Body as branches to the vine. We must also be able to meet Christ in the divine, continual act of creation, redemption and sanctification of the total universe. Christ's loving activity for us individually is discovered in an intuition of faith that reveals Him as the keystone to the multiple mystery of created being. In Him we discover the *Absolute*, the beginning and end of all unity in the cosmos. Faith gives us the eyes to see, not *what* God is but — in His personal, loving activity over the millennia for us, the destined children of God — *who* He is.

But to foster a steady growth of faith, an environment, a divine milieu, must be created in which Christ can be personally contacted. He is to be found at the root, the ground of our very existence. Teilhard insists that for the Christian with vision God, as Creator and more specifically as Redeemer, penetrates the world.[4]   It is not an epiphany, an appearance of God in the world, but a "diaphany" of God shining through the transparent world.

This Christ, diaphanously shining through the entire universe, is encountered in a loving act of surrender in which He becomes the *Thou*, complementing our *I*. Each Christian, now awakened to a new consciousness of Christ's universal presence, will discover his or her self-realization and full maturity in "being-with-Christ." Teilhard summarizes the key to the mystery of life very simply: "That which gives true value and happiness to existence is to lose oneself in another greater than oneself."[5]

To appreciate in greater detail the role of Christ in Teilhard's thought we must first see the broad outline of his spiritual vision, especially as presented in *The Divine Milieu*.

Creating A Divine Milieu

Teilhard himself tells us why he wrote *The Divine Milieu*. It was to be a book of piety presenting an ascetical or mystical doctrine that would be meaningful for the modern world.[6]

Teilhard was thinking of the people of his day torn between the evidence for evolution, and God's revelation about man's supernatural destiny. He felt drawn, even as was St. Francis Xavier, to bring the saving doctrine of Christ to the modern generation that was unable to see the reality behind sensory phenomena. The whole universe was exploding into ever greater multiplicity. But was there any unity beneath this increasing complexity? The immensity of the universe has caused a fear in the heart of modern man. It has dwarfed man into insignificance, sundered the narrow containers into which man had forced his throbbing world. A whole new concept of space-time is at the root of this disquiet. ". . . the 'malady of space-time' manifests itself as a rule by a feeling of futility, of being crushed by the enormities of the cosmos. . . . Sickness of the dead end, the anguish of feeling shut in. . . ."[7] To light the way out of this maze of enclosing, mechanistic fatalism, there suddenly flashed forth the astonishing vision of Teilhard de Chardin.

Behind the seemingly rigid determinism of matter, Teilhard discovers the delicate hand of the Holy Spirit giving order to the universe. For one who has faith to pierce beyond appearances, chance and hazard dissolve into an illusion. In the foreword to *The Phenomenon of Man*, Teilhard states his purpose: that men might *see* more and more beyond appearance to the inner order and finality of the physical cosmos. The human mind through reflection on the cosmic past and present can trace, he insists, the gradual unity in multiplicity in an ever progressive ascent that irreversibly produces a *cosmogenesis*, *biogenesis* and, finally, *anthropogenesis*. But only faith discovers a personal God permeating the universe with His conscious activity to bring the totality to a final point of convergence. *The Divine Milieu* is Teilhard's vision of faith that seeks not only to present God as the beginning and end of all order and perfection found in the universe, but also to outline in a practical way a plan whereby man can find God, loving and acting to bring him to his completion in Christ. Through a free act of love man can insert himself within this process and not only realize his own potentialities, (thus achieving happiness), but. in active cooperation with his Maker, help the whole universe move to its completion.

Mystique Of Action

The modern Christian lives in two worlds: the world of matter and the world of spirit. He is drawn by the beauties of this world and the challenge to make it an ever better place in which to live. His Christian *credo* tells him on the other hand that these ephemeral material beings will soon pass away and that he must lift his heart and his eyes heavenward. One cannot love God and mammon at the same time. Thus he feels a dual pull: one drawing him to full citizenship in the earthly city, the other recalling his future citizenship in the City of Heaven.

Christians have answered this dilemma in one of three ways. One can ignore and repress the desires for the things of this world and live for ''the things above'' by trying to flee from the present world. One can turn away from the evangelical summons (otherworldly values) and live completely in and for this world. Thirdly, one can try to compromise, attempting to now live for God, now for the world, never really resolving the dilemma.

Teilhard, in working out a mystique of action, insists that there is a fourth way. This consists in reconciling the tension between the love of God and of the world, between the desire for greater self-development and the striving for greater detachment from the things of this world.[8]

Spiritual writers all too often in the past presented work as a penance, a result of Original Sin. "You shall earn your bread by the sweat of your brow" (Gn 3:19).[9] Work was also presented as conflicting with love of God. By a pure intention of pleasing God, regardless of what one did, one could give his work a supernatural orientation. This spirituality conveyed the impression of a static world and a transcendent God outside of the material universe. Human activities had eternal value only as symbols of our submission to God. Man was on trial before the eternal Eye; his task consisted in learning how to do everything from the pure intention of pleasing God.

A Whole Process

Teilhard recognizes much truth in this traditional spirituality of work but seeks to complement it by seeing the whole material universe, with man at its center, from the viewpoint of God's finality. He strives to see man and his everyday work as an important part of God's plan wherein the past, present and future are dynamically interrelated, the whole process moving under God's personal activity to final completion. In *The Divine Milieu*, he insists that through the Incarnation nothing in the universe is "profane" for those who can see the inner presence of the resurrected Christ bringing the world to its consummation.[10] This vision is a gift of God that will allow us to see how all of our labors can be directed toward the building of the Kingdom of Heaven.

Teilhard insists that to have a pure intention to use creatures properly is not enough for sanctity in today's expanding universe. The glorious power of Christ's resurrection touches not only the soul of man but his body and the whole subhuman cosmos to "confer the hope of resurrection upon their bodies." Since the appearance of rational man, carrying in his intellect and will the image of his Maker, God evolves the universe and brings it to its completion through the instrumentality of human beings. Man is called to be a "co-creator," a "cooperator" with God in the transformation of the universe from seed to fruit, potency to act, imperfection to perfection. Therefore, it *does* matter what man does, for only through his action can he encounter God. Through his grace-infused soul man can touch the chaos of the material world and apply the Incarnation to it. The world can be spiritualized by man developing and using it according to the eternal mind of its Creator.[11]

St. Paul had pointed out how the incarnational activity of Christ was still going on in the universe. "For it pleased God the Father that in him all fullness should dwell, and that through him God should reconcile to himself every being, and make peace both on earth and in heaven through the blood shed on the cross" (Col 1:19-20).

Teilhard never forgot Paul's clear teaching that man was not by the mere fact of his natural existence called to be a "new creature" but that this renovation was completely due to God's gratuitous gift through Christ. He also never forgot Paul's clear injunction that God has entrusted to us the sacred priestly work of reconciling the cosmos in Christ (2 Cor 5:17-19).

Detachment

But human activities tend to flatter our sense of independence. How to keep the delicate balance between being a fully dependent creature, yet also a full "cooperator" with the divine Creator? Here Teilhard gives us his presentation of detachment and mortification which is in total harmony with the best in the Christian ascetical tradition. "Passionate indifference" is Teilhard's description of the Christian who has put on God's view of reality and has forgotten self as a point of reference and "in-centration."

Man's passivities, where he is an active recipient of God's gifts in all their manifestations, are the absolutely necessary means to keep his activities centered on God and free from any self-love. God acts in us through the passivities of growth whereby we have a built-in thirst for higher forms of life, for greater complexity within a greater integrated unity of experience. St. Irenaeus in the second century described it well by saying: "the glory of God is man living fully." A desire to participate more fully in life, in true being, is the urge that keeps us striving daily with ever-renewed energy.

The "joie de vivre" becomes such only when it is recognized as a haunting expression of God's loving invitation rooted deeply in the marrow of our being to "be perfect as your heavenly Father is perfect" (Mt 5:43). This is capable of fulfillment through our cooperation with God's activities in our lives. These activities and the "passivities of diminishment" are the two hands of God, the Son and the Holy Spirit, touching us in the external and internal events of each moment to bring us from the death of self-love to a new emerging life in the Trinity. The death of Christ on the cross had meaning only as a step to the restoration of His divine life to humanity through His glorified body. In the same way, the little crosses that come from either outside or from within have full meaning only as a purgation in order that Christ's image, according to which we have been created, may shine more brilliantly in us.

It is a universal law of nature that nothing lives but something dies; nothing dies but something lives. This sums up Teilhard's vision of the cross in the Christian life. But we do not merely shed imperfection for perfection, less life for more life, as static entities. Each advance to a form of being has a repercussion on the total perfection of the universe. No one with God's grace ever perfects him/herself without at the same time touching the world around them and raising it to a higher life. It is precisely through the activities and passivities of our daily life that we become a "new creation" along with the created world we now touch and change in Christ.

Transfigured Universe

Thus, development and renunciation are not opposed as antinomies. Attachment and detachment are necessary complements. The cross and resurrection are two phases of the seed maturing into the fruit. Matter and spirit, body and soul, evil and good, are all interrelated phases of a continuous progression in true, ontological life, the life that Christ came to give us in greater abundance. The unifying element is precisely that God in His immanence is in all His creatures, acting to fulfill them. Teilhard uses the example of Jacob who was awakened to perceive in a new way that the world around him was truly a holy place. The divine presence through the physical, created world "assails us, penetrates us and moulds us."

God is revealing Himself everywhere — through our groping efforts — as a universal milieu, an environment, the air that we breathe. All beings have full reality to the degree that they converge upon this Ultimate Point. God is the source of all perfections and the goal towards which created beings are moving in an *élan vital* to their completion.

This vision of worshipful communion between creature and Creator, whereby we lose ourselves in God as in an "Other," is grounded in the Word Incarnate, Jesus Christ. In Him, as St. Paul taught, all things are reunited and consummated. By the resurrectional presence of Christ who fills all things, the whole of creation has a meaningful consistency. [12]

By our actions, no matter how insignificant, we are building up the Body of Christ until it shall reach its consummation-Omega-Point in the *pleroma*, when Christ shall appear in His fullness of glory in the *parousia* and recapitulate under Himself as Head the whole created order.

All created beings are tied together in their thrust toward fulfillment. "Natures" of created beings, as conceived by Teilhard, are no longer the static, self-contained compartments of Aristotelian metaphysics. All matter is rushing in a "forward" and "upward" movement toward the Spirit. Divinity shoots through all of creation if only we would *see*.

In his work, *Super-Humanité, Super-Christ, Super-Charité*, Teilhard attempts to describe the interpenetration of the divine presence throughout all of reality. The mystics see all of reality surcharged with God; hence all of creation becomes lovable in God and "reciprocally God becomes knowable and lovable in all that surrounds us." No longer does the swirling, maddening multiplicity of creation take us away from God; the very created world becomes a "milieu" and a point of encounter for a universal communion between man and God.[13]

With Teilhard's spiritual vision as background, we can now examine the role Christ plays in it. The Christian, living in this divine milieu, sees beyond the phenomena of sense experience. Faith gives us the inner vision. "After a while" we can penetrate through surface impressions to perceive the inner logos, the meaning of each creature or event. We can see all creatures as events in the fulfillment of God's salvific designs.

But the greatest "event" for every Christian is always the encounter with the *Logos*, the Lord Jesus Christ Himself, in and through these same material creatures. He it is who gives reality to each being, who evolves the whole universe into the "new creation" foretold by St. Paul (2 Cor 5:17-19).

Cosmogenesis Through Evolution

Before we can study Teilhard's Christology, we must first understand his views of the evolution of the cosmos, since they are intimately connected. For Teilhard, the evolution of the world from greater complexity to greater consciousness ultimately results in the formation of the Christ-Body of the entire material world.

For Teilhard, all energy is psychic and is permeated by a divine spark of "amorizing" consciousness. Thus from the beginning of time there were two tendencies or manifestations of all energy: the *radial* and the *tangential*. Christopher Mooney describes these two energies: "Radial energy tends to draw an element forward into structures of greater complexity; tangential energy on the contrary tends to link an element to other elements on the same level of organization. In the early stages of the earth it was radial energy which led to the production of larger and more 'centered' molecules, until such time as the first 'critical point' of evolution was reached and there was the sudden appearance of life."[14]

Teilhard finds three constitutive elements of all creation. There is always a center as well as radial and tangential energies. He relates the tangential to what he calls the WITHOUT of things and the radial to the WITHIN. All created, material beings possess a Without and a Within. Science has made great strides in studying the Without. It is only beginning to scratch the surface of the Within of things.

Evolution for Teilhard is nothing more than the interaction of the Without and the Within, of the tangential and radial energies in accordance with the Law of Complexity-Consciousness. This means that the more complex an organic structure is (bringing about a greater internal unity and hence the power of concentration), there will also be in direct proportion a higher degree of consciousness.

In *The Phenomenon of Man* Teilhard painstakingly traced his cosmogenesis from the first created proton to human life: the *noosphere*. Man, at last, stood above all the other creatures and cried out, "I alone know and I know that I know." No other animal has man's unquenchable longing for eternal life. He alone can turn within himself and reflect on the purpose of his being and his relation to all other beings. He can penetrate the mystery of life, discover the purpose behind this movement of evolving multiplicity, and even foster or hinder the process.

Complexity-Consciousness

Teilhard's *law of complexity* states that matter is always moving to higher forms of greater complexity in molecular structure with a proportionate development in consciousness. In his work, *Comment Je Crois*, Teilhard confesses that he is aware of an interior movement that animates the whole universe as well as each of its parts. This movement is "towards Spirit."[15]

Teilhard loved matter because he always saw it in its movement towards the spiritual. When man developed the power of reflection, a living being became the center of personalization. This personalized creature evolves from a self-centered being intent on self-preservation, to a being going out through communication and a conscious act of love for "another self." This evolutionary process unites humanity into a unity of multiple complexity and differentiation.

For Teilhard there were three "quantum" jumps in radial energies that evolved into something completely different from the original elements. The first quantum leap was the birth of life, the first living cell. Some evidence indicates that the virus, which is a megamolecule exhibiting the properties of a living cell only when it is near *DNA*, may constitute that link between life and pre-life.

The second quantum jump occurred with the birth of the first grain of thought. From the *biosphere* there came forth the *noosphere*, the appearance of thinking humanity. Here, evolution became conscious of itself. Even though the Law of Complexity-Consciousness continues to operate, man's newly acquired ability to reflect has given him the choice of "temporarily" (and this could mean millions of years or a short span of time) diverting the direction of evolution. Evolution is no longer deterministic. It can be affected by human beings.

Christogenesis

For Teilhard the third quantum jump took place two thousand years ago in the Incarnation of Jesus Christ. In Teilhard's terminology this was the movement of the *noosphere* into the *Christosphere*. The "hyperpersonal" has evolved.[16] This hyperpersonal grain claims a relationship with the first grain of the stuff of the universe. It declares a paradox: to love one's enemies, even to lay down one's life for them. It recognizes that what unites is only love; it becomes the lowest in going down the ladder of evolution in order to experience all the steps by which we have ascended, namely, death. This hyperpersonal grain recognized its mission as uniting, through death, the lowest levels of the cosmos with the highest, the Alpha and the Omega. The radial energy, that of the tangential and the center now have become a single point in the person of Jesus Christ.

What is this point of union and convergence toward which all matter, all human beings are moving? The process of moving together through space and time is likened by Teilhard to a cone. The tip or point of the cone he calls Omega. This is the goal towards which evolution is moving, the point of convergence of all inferior lines which meet in it.

Before Teilhard identifies this Omega Point with Christ, he describes it in greater detail. The ultimate point drawing not only all human beings but all the universe shows three characteristics: (1) It must be of an objective nature; it cannot be a mere figment of man's imagination. As the process of evolution and the laws of its development are real, so too must be the end towards which it is moving. (2) It must have the power in itself to draw, by its own activity, all creatures into a unity to their full consummation. In order to draw intellectual beings, this point of attraction must also be an intellectual being, a person. But if this person draws other persons he must do this through his own power and goodness. Ultimately, this is done through the act of love by which a person draws another into the highest union of self-communication. (3) It must be able to move the whole universe to its united perfection without any fear of regression, destruction or total frustration.[17]

Jesus Christ Is The Omega Point

What follows in Teilhard's thinking has received much criticism from those who have followed him up to this point. When he seeks to clarify and "incarnate" the Omega Point he is accused of having left science and entered the realm of mysticism. His reasoning can be stated thus: Man has evolved, and his highest perfection in the individual consciousness is his power of self-reflection. The total progress of humanity can likewise be measured by the conjoined reflection of united human beings. Thus, in the process of evolution through a progressive, irreversible movement of diverse elements, convergence must be a real, existing point of unity. It must be a person who exists, yet transcends all other finite, inferior forms. This person is not caused by the convergence of humanity but is the moving force that converges by drawing the human race into a real unity around this center of attraction. This person is spiritual, since he attracts other spiritual beings as their fulfillment. He must be eternal and transcendent, the fullness of being, never adding to his being but possessing all perfections desired by mankind in its ever growing thirst for more being, for a richer and more intense life. This person, finally, must be immanent. Only because this person transcends *all* finite being is he capable of being immanent to *each* being. But there is only one person who has been inserted into the human race and is capable of drawing other human beings by a human act of love, yet who remains completely transcendent to all people. This person must be infinite in order to command the aspirations of all people for all times. But the only infinite person drawn from the human race is Jesus Christ, the God-Man.

In his work, *Super-Humanité, Super-Christ, Super-Charité*, Teilhard identifies this Omega Point with Christ. By taking upon Himself a human nature, Christ becomes the perfect human being, "humanity appeared." But, as Christ also actively consummates the totality and fullness of humanity, He is "super-humanity appeared." Christ is the Omega Point, capable of attracting other human beings to their fulfillment.[18]   Teilhard does not wish to speak of another Christ, a second Christ, different from the first who lived historically in space and time, who "dwelt among us." He intends to speak of the same Christ, the eternal Christ who discloses Himself to us under a new form and a new dimension.

In his work, *The Phenomenon of Man*, Teilhard unmistakably identifies the historical Christ with the converging point of all evolution. He is drawing to Himself the total "psychism" of the earth until that time when all will be transformed into God, to use St. Paul's words.[19]   But in that final consummation of all things in God, our individuality will not be swallowed up into divinity as pantheism teaches. Each element, retaining its own proper identity, will reach its full perfection by being united with the Omega Point.

The Cosmic Christ

Teilhard's starting point, as we have seen, is the evolutionary process which he considers as proven fact. He projects this process into the future with his theory of the ever-converging universe, moving with greater affinity to Spirit. Into this hypothesis he injects his Christian faith based on revelation, especially St. John and St. Paul. Science and religious faith comprise two different sources of knowledge, but do not contradict each other, as the Positivists maintain. They are facets of truth leading to the same Center.

But it might be legitimately asked: If the cosmic Christ coincides with the development of the cosmogenesis, does not the historical Christ disappear? Is the cosmic Christ, the Omega Point, merely a poetic description of the gradual unfolding of the law of cosmic evolution? Teilhard's expressions at times would lead us dangerously close to such a conclusion. In his essay, *Comment Je Crois*, he insists that mankind is consummated with and attains to the total Christ only at the end of evolution. In such expressions, do not the historical acts of Christ's Incarnation, Redemption, Resurrection and Ascension seem to be unimportant, even unnecessary?

Teilhard repeatedly insists that his cosmic Christ is the Christ of the Gospels. In *The Divine Milieu* he equates St. Paul's recapitulating, universal Christ with the same flesh-and-blood Christ who was born of Mary and who died on the cross. Without this identity with the historical person of Jesus Christ, he realizes that he would be in the company of the wildest-eyed visionaries and illuminati.[21]

Superficial readers of Teilhard are apt to confuse his two sources of knowledge, the laws of scientific evolution and those of divine revelation. They thus erroneously conclude that Teilhard was destroying the gratuity of the supernatural order by making the fulfillment of each creature in the final *pleroma* a matter of mere cosmogenesis. In an early work, his *Milieu Mystique* (1917), Teilhard clearly distinguishes between what is due to nature and what is a purely gratuitous gift of God. Yet he points out how Christ builds, by transformation, this supernatural structure upon natural perfection.

Teilhard, in his essay *Mon Univers*, looked at the universe as having only one Center which operated on both levels with distinction, the natural and the supernatural. This Center was moving creation both to greater consciousness and to the highest degree of sanctity. This Center, he insists, is Jesus Christ, both in His historical person as well as in His projected glorified person in the cosmos.[22]

In one of his brief interchanges of letters with the Christian existential philosopher, Maurice Blondel, Teilhard more explicitly tells us how he views the interrelationship of the natural and supernatural levels of being. The supernatural fullness of Christ is being formed by the re-creation of the natural. Christ gives Himself to us to the degree that the world is more fully and more naturally developed.[23]

Teilhard stresses that through the Incarnation, the Divine Word has inserted Himself within our material "natural" universe. He has become the cosmic Center drawing all beings (now elevated by the gratuitous loving activity of God) to a united destiny around Himself, the Omega Point.

Cosmic Or Christic "Nature"

Teilhard was convinced that the total material universe is in movement toward a greater unified convergence in consciousness, a hyper-personalized organism. He was as sure of this as he was of the truths of the Christian revelation concerning the building up of the Mystical Body and the recapitulation of all things in Jesus Christ. He complains in *Le Christique*, another of his unedited works (1955), that up to the present, despite the dominant place that St. Paul gives it, the third aspect or third "nature" of Christ (that is, His "cosmic" function in the universe) has not been given sufficient consideration by theologians. He is not talking about a new third nature in the strict sense of the word as opposing the human and divine. With the convergence of human experiences allowing us to see a unity within so much multiplicity, Teilhard insists that it is time for Christianity to awaken to a distinct consciousness of this third dimension or function of Christ.

In times past, Christ's relationship to the material universe (often conceived as a static cosmos) was understood in a juridical way. He was King over all creation because He was declared to be such. There was little reflection on any organic dependent relation of creation upon Him.[24]

Earlier, in the written summary of his personal views entitled

Comment Je Vois (published in 1948), Teilhard used the term "Christic nature" but with somewhat more caution. He distinguished between the preexisting Word on the one hand and the historical, incarnate Man Jesus on the other. Between these two aspects, Teilhard distinguishes (as he did in *Le Christique*) a sort of emergent "third nature," one that is Christic (he adds the words: "if I dare to say so! . . ."). This is the aspect of Christ that St. Paul writes about, the full, total Christ whose activity consists precisely in "recapitulation," in bringing the universe to its ultimate center through the transforming energies of His resurrection.[25]

We have already pointed out that Teilhard did not believe in a third nature distinct and different from the two natures, divine and human, that make up the total, historical person, Jesus Christ. In his use of the term "cosmic" or "christic nature," Teilhard did not intend to give a metaphysical definition of a new and distinct nature, existing outside of the gloriously resurrected Jesus Christ. Teilhard stresses Christ's new and ever-growing relation with the created cosmos in a phenomenological and mystical way through a real, "physical" relationship. Thus he strongly emphasizes the building up of the Mystical Body of Christ, as a physical third "nature." Teilhard complains in his *La Vie Cosmique* that St. Paul's strong analogy of the Body of Christ has theologically been interpreted more often as a social agglomeration and not as Paul had envisioned it, as a natural organism. He claims that the Body of Christ, in the doctrine of St. Paul, St. John and the Church Fathers, meant a living and moving organism whose members were united in a physical and biological sense.[26]

It has been pointed out in reference to the above quotation that Teilhard uses the words "nature," "physically" and "biologically" quite loosely. It is precisely his christology that most of his critics have attacked. But he has told his readers that his thoughts were not always complete nor expressed in precise language. The great confusion comes from his eagerness to present his picture of the evolution of all created natures climaxing gradually in their fulfillment in Christ as the One who completes Himself in completing them.[27]

Physical Center

St. John taught that "all things came into being through him (Christ, the Logos) and without him there came to be not one thing that has come to be" (Jn 1:3); St. Paul taught that in Christ "God shall be all in all" (1 Cor 15:28); "All things have been created through him (Christ) and for him . . . and in him they are all preserved in being" (Col 1:16-17); "He it is who fills all things" (Col 2:19). These and other texts (such as Ep 4:10 and Col 3:11) were sufficient doctrinal basis, Teilhard thought, to take Christ, the personalized Omega Point of the universe, as the literal physical Center of the cosmos. He boldly asserts in his essay, *Super-Humanité, Super-Christ, Super-Charité*, that if we were to take the daring statements of St. Paul literally, then Christ would appear to us as the Omega Point of convergence and there would follow a whole series of marvelous properties as qualities of His risen humanity.[28]

What does Teilhard mean when he says that Christ is literally the physical Center of this expanding universe? Was this hyperbole or did Teilhard really mean that Christ forms sort of a "physical" bond with other human beings in this world? Certainly the frequency of his use of the word "physical" would imply that he meant it literally. Most modern people think of "physical" as synonymous with "material," hence in opposition to "spiritual." But Teilhard's "physical" must be seen in the context of his own thought and system.

Physical, as used by Teilhard, has some of the nuance and breadth of the term as used by the early Greek Fathers. *Physis* means "nature," but not in the strictly metaphysical sense. Perhaps "reality" or "ontological reality" would be a better way to translate Teilhard's sense of *physical*, for it signifies, not only a

given being in its present existence, but above all it includes the
total being in its dynamic progression towards fulfillment. Its
perfect fulfillment coincides with God's finality which is the
purpose for His immanent activity in creatures. An essential con-
tribution to the full "reality" of a given human being is the
continuity that joins the Head and members, Christ and us, and
effects the individual divinization which is our fullness, flowing
out into the collective divinization.

The Eucharist

But still there seems to be an element missing, the bond of
union. How does man make contact with Christ, the Center of the
universe? How can we encounter Christ? The sacrament of the
Eucharist is for Teilhard the chief bond of contact, of union
between the Incarnate Word, Christ, and an individual human
person. The Eucharist is shorn, however, of the false overtones of
self-centered, individualistic pietism. It is presented in the context
of an evolving, expanding universe that is moving always under the
guiding hand of the cosmic Christ towards an ever greater consciousness and convergence or centricity through love. In *Le
Milieu Mystique*, Teilhard writes, "I discovered that everything
was again centered upon a Point, upon a Person, and this Person
was You, Jesus!. . From the moment that you said 'This is My
Body,' not only the bread on the altar, but to a certain extent
everything in the universe that nourishes in our souls the life of
grace and the spirit became Yours."[29]
From the consecrated species of bread and wine wherein is
contained, in space and time, the physical Body-Person of Jesus
Christ, a "universal transubstantiation" is taking place. Christ's
transforming activity moves from the church's altar to the altar of
the material universe. In *Le Christique* Teilhard develops this
insight by describing, through the eyes of faith, how the transubstantiation of bread and wine into the eucharistic Body and Blood

of Jesus Christ is extended into the converging world to include the totality of all the joys and pains that result from the convergence process. The words of consecration fall over these and thus render possible a universal communion.

The Church — A Phylum Of Love

Teilhard envisions the Church as the "place" where Christ, the Center of the universe, meets His followers and transforms them into Himself through the Holy Spirit of love. "Love differentiates as it unites" is Teilhard's keen insight into the essence of a loving community, hence of the Church of Christ, His Mystical Body.

Teilhard usually does not stress the Church as a community founded by Jesus Christ with a given hierarchical structure and a collective unity in faith, sacraments and teaching magisterium. Allowing for the institutional elements, he focuses rather on its dynamic aspect — the "core" concept of the members transformed by the incarnational activity of Christ in their lives. Through the intensity of lives lived "in Christ Jesus," by purity, faith and fidelity, they converge to "form Christ." He expresses this in strong terms in *The Divine Milieu*.[30]   Whatever we do or suffer with faith and love makes us a more integral part of Christ's Mystical Body. These actions are not only turned to good; they are turned into Christ.

Through this body of christified persons, Christ reaches the rest of mankind and the material universe. To Teilhard, the growing Body-Person Christ is a "phylum of salvation," an organized collectivity that spreads its inner life and hyper-personalism in a movement of greater consciousness, always ascending until the completion of the Body in the *parousia*. Teilhard summarizes this at the conclusion of his work, *The Phenomenon of Man*. He compares the Christian "leaven" to a *phylum* that, through greater consciousness, moves towards a unity effected by love. This consciousness reaches its fullness in the spiritual relationship of love to the transcendent pole of the whole universal process of convergence, Jesus Christ.[31]

The Church as a growing phenomenon is like a biological phylum, all of whose members have a common set of characteristics distinguishing them from members of other phyla. This *body* of members grows in an ascent of greater consciousness, freedom and reflection, synthesized by the Christian act of fraternal love.

The source and object of this common *agape* is the Omega Point, the cosmic Christ. The christic energy of grace deepens the reflective consciousness of the highly individuated members into a convergence by a hyper-personal love of each towards Christ-Omega and towards one another. Love, Teilhard points out, is the "within" of things, the immanent force unifying all conscious beings, "personalizing" by totalizing.

No truly personalized union between rational beings is possible without love. Love alone can unite people and fulfill them. In *The Phenomenon of Man*, Teilhard asks: If in our love relationship with another we find our truest "person," why should it not be true also on a world-wide dimension?[32]

In spite of the tragic events of the twentieth century, Teilhard's optimism and deep Christian faith drove him on to assert that the Church, this phylum of love, would continue to expand, unleashing men's ability to be more personalized by becoming more reflectively conscious in their love-motivated activities.

Teilhard's Christological Contribution

Teilhard would have been the last to claim that his christology was original. His frequent appeals to St. Paul, St. John and the early Fathers indicate his respect for the traditional mind of the Church. Yet his approach to christology is not the traditional approach of the majority of dogmatic theologians. From his scientific background, he brought to his treatment of christology not only profound respect for empirical methodology but a new per-spective — that of cosmic evolution.

He deeply felt the schism between science and faith, the dichotomy between modern life with its immersion in material tasks, and the spiritual life. By approaching christology through the perspective of cosmic evolution, he tried to create a synthesis of scientific, theological and philosophical knowledge.

Jean Danielou[33] has pointed out how Teilhard sought to correct the static concept of man by returning to the dynamic Biblical view of his three-dimensional unity: (1) Man becomes master of the cosmos and actuates the divine image within himself by his work, his actual daily labors. (2) He moves through his work and social relationships into a community of interpersonalism based on love, and through love of neighbor he ascends to love of God. (3) Thus, both as an individual and as a member of a community, man opens his whole being to adoration of God, his Maker and final end.

Teilhard's optimism finds a way to unite these three stages, so that the technical world of man's daily activities is shown as the "stuff" out of which the community in Christ is formed to give adoration through the whole universe to God. The Incarnation is, of course, the heart of his cosmic christology. At the decisive moment in the evolutive process of the universe (more specifically, of man in the noosphere), God becomes man. Christ is the Speech of God telling us of His plans. He is the key to the mysterious ways of God that unfold in the perspective of cosmic evolution. He is the climax, perfect man, everything human beings are groaning to become, the fulfillment of the human race.

Christ Is Humanity Fulfilled

Jesus Christ is humanity fulfilled. He is the image according to which all human beings have been created. But He is also the means or axis along which man moves to the higher and last step of evolution, to *christogenesis*. As St. Paul wrote: ''And this good pleasure he decreed to put into effect in Christ when the designated period of time had elapsed, namely, to gather all creation both in heaven and on earth under one Head, Christ'' (Ep 1:9-10). Teilhard is telling the modern world that Christ, immersed in the evolving cosmos, is actively guiding this world to Himself as the Omega Point of reconciliation with His heavenly Father.

Science and faith blend as complementary reports of the presence of God actively working to fulfill His universe. Science sees in this divine activity an unfathomable object of intricately ordered matter and energy. Faith reveals that this activity proceeds from a divine, intensely personal love towards the human race. Faith discovers the Divine Milieu that is this unfolding Love in the smile of a child, in the steady rhythm of the subway, in the water drop that mirrors His wondrous, turbulent world thrusting toward completion.

Man is to hear the Speech of God, Christ, in every creature as it groans its way to greater perfection. But, sadly, he can close his ears. But when he does turn away, he imprisons himself in the deaf egoism which produces self-destruction. Thus the process of the evolving universe goes forward and upward at the same time. And inserted within this total process, guided always by Christ to the fullness which will presage His *parousia*, is that phylum of salvation, the Church — those members of Christ who, through death to self, detachment and the cross, have rendered themselves ''passionately indifferent'' to everything but Christ.

Christ is being formed in them in a very real, ontological way as they yield themselves more perfectly to His direction. Charged with the living presence of Christ within them, these christified people hasten the day when the evolving universe and the evolving Christ in His members will converge in the Omega Point. Then He will truly be ''all things in all.'' ''For it pleased God the Father that in him all fullness should dwell, and that through him God should reconcile to himself every being, and make peace both on earth and in heaven through the blood shed on the cross'' (Col 1:19-20).

ENDNOTES

1 Teilhard de Chardin: *Réflexions sur la probabilité scientifique*, 1951, in: *L'Activation de l'energie* (Paris: Editions du Seuil, 1963), p. 282.

2 Much of what is contained in this chapter can be found in greater development in my book: *The Cosmic Christ, From Paul to Teilhard* (N.Y.: Sheed & Ward, 1968), pp. 182-220. Some leading works on Teilhard's ideas are the following: Neville Braybrooke, ed.; *Teilhard de Chardin: Pilgrim of the Future* (N.Y.: Seabury Press, 1964); Louis Cognet: *Le Père Teilhard de Chardin et la pensée contemporaine* (Paris: Flammarion, 1952); George Crespy: *La Pensée théologique de Teilhard de Chardin* (Paris: Editions Universitaires, 1961); Claude Cuenot: *Teilhard de Chardin* (Baltimore: Helicon Press, 1956 [contains a complete bibliography]); Henri de Lubac: *The Religion of Teilhard de Chardin* (N.Y.: Désclée, 1967); Robert Faricy: *Teilhard de Chardin's Theology of the Christian in the World* (N.Y.: Sheed & Ward, 1967); Robert Francoeur, ed.: *The World of Teilhard* (Baltimore: Helicon, 1961); Christopher Mooney: *Teilhard de Chardin and the Mystery of Christ* (N.Y.: Harper, 1966); Michael Murray: *The Thought of Teilhard de Chardin* (N.Y.: Seabury Press, 1966); Oliver Rabut: *Teilhard de Chardin: A Critical Study* (N.Y.: Sheed & Ward, 1961); Charles Raven: *Teilhard de Chardin, Scientist and Seer* (N.Y.: Harper, 1962); Emile Rideau: *La Pensée du Père Teilhard de Chardin* (Paris: Editions du Seuil, 1965); Pierre Smulders: *The Design of Teilhard de Chardin* (Westminster, MD: Newman, 1967); Claude Tresmontant: *Pierre Teilhard de Chardin* (Baltimore: Helicon Press, 1959); N.M. Wildiers: *Teilhard de Chardin* (Paris: Editions Universitaires, 1960); Robert Hale: *Christ and the Universe* (Chicago: Franciscan Herald Press, 1972).

3 Teilhard de Chardin: *The Divine Milieu*; tr. by B. Wall, et al. (London: Collins Sons & Co. and N.Y.: Harper & Row, 1960), p. 14.

4 Ibid., pp. 94-110.

5 *Letters from a Traveller*; tr. by B. Wall, et al. (N.Y.: Harper, 1962), p. 264.

6 Ibid., pp. 133-134.

7 *The Phenomenon of Man*, tr. by Bernard Wall (N.Y.: Harper Torchbooks, 1959), pp. 226, 228.

8 *The Divine Milieu*, p. 21.

9 Adam worked before the Fall, but after the Fall his work was associated with hardship and exertion — "sweat."

10 *The Divine Milieu*, p. 23.

11 Ibid., p. 89.

12 Ibid., p. 101.

13 *Super-Humanité, Super-Christ, Super-Charité, in: Oeuvres de Pierre Chardin*, Vol. 9 (Paris: Seuil, 1965), p. 213. English translation found in: *Science and Christ* (N.Y.: Harper & Row, 1968), p. 153.

14 C. Mooney: *Teilhard de Chardin and the Mystery of Christ* (Garden City, N.Y.: Doubleday, 1968), p. 44.

15 *Comment Je Crois*, Engl. translation is found in: *Christianity and Evolution* (N.Y.: Harcourt, Brace, Jovanovich, 1971), p. 99.
16 I am indebted to Dr. Mark Shamany, an engineer and Teilhardian scholar, for this term and his explanation in various conversations we have had.
17 *The Future of Man*, tr. by N. Denny (N.Y.: Harper, 1964), pp. 82-89.
18 *Super-Humanité*, p. 209.
19 A reference to St. Paul's Greek expression: "en pasi pana theos" in 1 Cor 15:28.
20 *The Phenomenon of Man*, p. 294.
21 *The Divine Milieu*, p. 95.
22 *Mons Univers* (1924); in *Oeuvres*; Vol. 9 (Paris: Seuil, 1965), pp. 85-94.
23 Cf. Letter of Dec. 12, 1919, *Archives de Philosophie*, 24 (1961), pp. 139-140.
24 Cf. *Le Christique* (1955), unpublished.
25 *Comment Je Vois* (1948), unedited.
26 *La Vie Cosmique, Ecrits du Temps de la Guerre, 1916-1919* (Paris: Grasset, 1965), pp. 39-40, 47.
27 *Super-Humanité*, p. 211.
28 Ibid.
29 *Le Milieu Mystique* (1917), p. 23, cited by C. Mooney: "Anxiety in Teilhard de Chardin," in: *Thought*, (Winter, 1964), p. 520.
30 *The Divine Milieu*, p. 101.
31 *The Phenomenon of Man*, p. 298.
32 Ibid., p 298.
33 Jean Danielou: "Signification de Teilhard de Chardin," in: *Etudes* (February, 1962), p. 161.

CHAPTER

7

God's Emptying Love

In this intoxicating world of exploding energy, we desperately need to learn the only lesson that we are here to learn and live by. We have all too long fashioned God according to our own image. We seek our identity in power and self-containment. We believe that happiness will be ours when we are independent and powerful. We believe that absolute control — with no ignorance, no mystery, no need to trust anyone — is the key to success.

We have accepted Nietzsche as our guide who teaches us that the will to power is the key to fulfillment.[1] We act on his teaching that all that proceeds from power is good and all that springs from weakness is bad.[2] In religion we believe "in God the Father almighty, Creator of heaven and earth." Jesus Christ is proved to be God because He worked powerful miracles that defied God's natural laws, the greatest being His resurrection.

The God we have forgotten from Scripture is the one revealed to us in the *Ebed Yahweh*, the Suffering Servant of God, Jesus Christ How few of us understand that God is God, not *because* He possesses absolute power, but *that* He is absolute love! "Power comes to full strength in weakness" (2 Cor 12:9). God's nature is shown in His loving power to share His life with His creatures.

Made in God's image and likeness (Gn 1:26), we need to know
who God really is, what He is like, in order to know who we are and
how we can be happy. If we can understand that God so loves us as
to give us His only begotten Son (Jn 3:16), then the Incarnation is
no longer God merely taking upon Himself our humanity. It becomes above all an emptying, a *kenosis*, out of perfect, humble,
self-sacrificing love so that we can share in His life and richness.

Let us see how this chapter fits into the preceding ones. We
have first outlined a new vision. This, we said, is not really new for
it is the dynamic vision presented in the Bible. In it, God dynamically interacts with His created world, especially with human
beings who share His very own image and likeness — who can
know personalized love and return it by a willed commitment in
loving obedience. God is not only transcendent and "other" than
His creation; He freely wills to be the "inside" presence of loving
activity in each creature. In such a view, the Cartesian dichotomy
between a thinking person and an objective, static world is
meaningless.

We looked at nuclear physics and discovered a world like that
presented in Scripture. The old Newtonian world view proved to be
inadequate, with its static image of God, man and the created
cosmos. It is being replaced with a new physics showing the
changing world of interrelationships and new and evolving forms
of energy. Nothing is static; nothing is unrelated to the otherness of
things.

We turned to modern process-theologians who seek to offset
"traditional theism" by presenting a dynamic view of God in
intimate relationships with man. All things and events are occasions for God to become complete as God, in cooperation with
man's creative free choices, to co-create an exciting, ever-
changing world.

The chapter on the early Greek Fathers presented mystics
rooted in Scripture and their own personal experiences of a God
who is both awesome and transcendent, yet tender and intimate in

His immanence within us. We explored in two chapters their apophetic approach to a knowledge that went beyond intellection. It is a knowledge of knowing by not-knowing, an experience given by God to the humble and the pure of heart. God is experienced, not in His unchangeable essence, but in His uncreated energies of love, His personalized relations as unique Father, Son and Holy Spirit. Grace, for these Fathers, becomes primarily God emptying Himself as self-gift to us out of His unfolding love in the context of each moment.

Pierre Teilhard de Chardin, the Jesuit paleontologist and mystic, unites the biblical and patristic view with modern physics to show us a vision of the cosmic Christ, inside of all creation and bringing the entire cosmos into a unity of love with human cooperation.

Now we wish to concentrate on the presence of God as humble, kenotic (or self-emptying), creative love. True power in God and in us will be shown to consist in love manifested in self-sacrificing compassion for the "other."

An Earthy God

The biblical God is an earthy God. He loves His created world. He has freely created it out of His emptying love that He wishes to share with His creatures. They become not only the "other" to which God can relate as source and end, but creatures in whom God is immanently present, giving of Himself in active creativity. God sees that His world is "very good" (Gn 1:18), because He is the ground of being for all His creatures. He by creation empties Himself of His isolation and is now able to relate as an "other" to His creatures. Jesus taught that His Father is always actively working out of love for all His creatures. "My Father goes on working and so do I" (Jn 5:17).

The late Abraham Joshua Heschel, one of America's leading Jewish theologians, in his work *The Prophets*, uses the word *pathos* to describe God's "being in a personal and intimate relation to the world . . . a loving care, a dynamic relation between God and the world . . . (God's) constant concern and involvement . . . an emotional engagement."[3]

From Scripture, we see that God is a pursuing Lover. His love is demonstrated by His involvement with His beloved children. Therefore, He is vulnerable, humble, waiting, ready to suffer the insolence and indifference of mankind.[4]

God is generous in His loving activities. He wishes to communicate Himself to mankind, to each of us, by self-emptying love — a self-gift that moves to communion with His human creatures. But precisely because He is so immediately present and immanently inside of each person, each creature, God can also "suffer." He must also run the awesome risk of giving love and being rejected, at least by angels and human beings. This is not a "negative" darkness in God nor is it an "imperfection" that makes God dependent upon His own creatures to supplant some deficiency in His nature. This is God's humble, free choice to share Himself as gift to His own creatures. This is a positive aspect of darkness, the possibility of relationships in which both God and His human creatures accept the risk of the undefined, the not-yet. This is God's love manifesting itself in a different way than that manifested within the Trinity itself.

An Absent God

Today, for many people, God is too ethereal to have "real" existence or at least vital meaning for their lives. In our technological world man, not God, is the center. Man has built science into an idol, thinking that it can solve all problems.

Yet such egocentrism has dehumanized us. We have turned inwardly to focus upon ourselves as the center of all thoughts and values. We have largely lost the sense of transcendence, the ability to move outward to live for others. Self-sacrificing love is a lost art.

We crave such love but lack the discipline to find our true identity in living for another in true self-giving. We do not know how or even why we should break down the walls that separate us from others.

As a result, people become more violent and self-assertive, while finding less and less meaning to life. The existentialist philosopher, Jean-Paul Sartre, assures us that there is no exit from the absurdity of existence. One truth is certain for Sartre — other people are hell!

Christian Humanism

We moderns are searching for the answer to the haunting question: "What does it mean to be a human person?" Only when we can answer this and live by the correct answer will we be able to ask: "Who is God for us?"

For Christians, Jesus Christ is what it means to be human. But it is in Him and the example He gave that we can understand how God is in the lives of modern people. In the Gospels Jesus shows us how we can live a transcendent love that is a self-emptying sacrifice for others. He lives for others, to bring fullness to the poor, the sick, the outcasts of society, the oppressed and the discriminated against, the criminals and the sinners.

Mad Generosity

Jesus, gentle and kind, told those whom He met that if they were to become rich, they would have to give everything away and in emptiness they would be filled. They would have to lose their lives to find meaning in life. Jesus' disciples would have to live as He did, giving away their lives for love of one another. He was the "friend of sinners" and went about doing good. He turned the other cheek and forgave His enemies in unrequited love. To the sick and the disturbed He brought comfort and healing. He was meek and humble and wanted no part of Caesar's or the world's power. The only power He possessed was to love each person as uniquely beautiful in His Father's creative love. He touched the crowds, listened to their anxieties, forgave their sins. He lived only to bring life, and that more abundantly (Jn 10:10), to all who wanted to receive such life. He was totally available to all who needed and accepted Him.

Jesus had few disciples because many thought He was mad — or at least very "impractical." Many, like the rich young man (Mk 10:17-22), walked away from Him. His talk about taking up one's "cross" and following Him found even fewer takers.

His language sounded extravagant, unreal and impractical. If you had an eye that scandalized you, you were to gouge it out. If you really had faith, you could walk up to a mountain and tell it to jump into the sea and it would do just that. We were to visit the sick, the lonely, the prisoners and tell them that we loved them. We were to be concerned and caring for all who were in need — bodily, mentally and spiritually — because that was the way the Heavenly Father loved each of us. We were to give and give, even losing our lives for others. We were to be servants to everyone, washing their feet, going the extra mile and giving, not only the coat, but the very shirt off our backs to a needy neighbor. Whatever we did to any person, we did to God!

A New Humanism

The Second Vatican Council's *Constitution on the Church in the Modern World* challenges not only Catholics but all humanity to enter into a new humanism by seeing that to live as Christ lived is to become human:

> *The truth is that only in the mystery of the Incarnate Word does the mystery of man take on light. For Adam, the first man, was a figure of him who was to come, namely, Christ*

the Lord. Christ, the final Adam, by the revelation of the mystery of the Father and his love, fully reveals man to man himself and makes his supreme calling clear. . . . Again, whoever follows after Christ the perfect man becomes himself more of a man.[5]

God is not far away from us. He is to be encountered as an actively concerned, loving Father in our growing responsibility for every human person and for the fulfillment of this material creation. Gregory Baum well expresses this christological humanism which is at bottom the discovery of the divine in the human. "For in Christ is revealed to us who man shall be or, more carefully, who the transcendent dynamism is by which, gratuitously, all men are summoned and freed to become more fully human. Divine grace recreates in men the perfect humanity revealed in Christ. Christianity is humanistic in the sense that it reveals, celebrates, and promotes the entry of all men into greater likeness to Jesus Christ."[6]

What is explicitly true of Christ is implicitly true of every human being. Our personal history is the "place" where we are to meet God as our Creator and Redeemer. It is only in the context of our human situation that we are to experience God as Jesus did in His human life. Only there can we grow in transcendent, compassionate love shown toward our neighbor.

The Good News of Christianity is not only that Jesus Christ is the perfect human being by the way He lived and acted in society, but that He is also the way God lives and acts in relationship to us and our world. Jesus said: "As the Father has loved me, so I have loved you" (Jn 15:9). In Jesus Christ, God and man are in complementary, personal relationships. We become more human in full freedom and transcendent happiness and meaningfulness when we love as Jesus lived. Jesus images for us in human form the emptying love of God on our behalf in each moment of our lives.

Entering Into The Kingdom Of God

We begin with the historical Jesus of the Gospels in order to reach the Christ of faith. By His resurrectional power we are able to participate in His kenotic or self-emptying love in service to others. He leads us as ''the Way, the Truth and the Life'' (Jn 14:6) to know and experience the inner nature of God as self-emptying love.

Jesus actualized God's emptying love for us by His actions. What is God like? He is like Jesus. The authority with which Jesus taught convinced those who accepted Him that He knew the nature of the Father. Jesus' preaching centered on the Kingdom of God. His disciples came to realize that He was bringing that Kingdom about by His teachings and style of life.

But His teaching about God's Kingdom was so different from what His contemporaries expected it to be. They all too easily forgot the suffering servant theme in Isaiah. Peter, James and John were not so eager to follow a Leader who would have to suffer and die in order to enter into His glorious Kingdom. At first, they wanted power and glory, the first seats of honor in the Kingdom. They did not want to embrace humiliations, poverty, humble service to the least, to turn the cheek, to do no violence, to call no one enemy.

If the Kingdom message is so central to the Gospel, we must understand what Jesus meant by it. Alfred North Whitehead claimed that Jesus' message was very quickly distorted when Christianity was officially accepted as the religion of the Roman Empire:

> *When the Western world accepted Christianity, Caesar conquered. . . The brief Galilean vision of humility flickered throughout the ages, uncertainly. In the official formulation of religion, it has assumed the trivial form of the mere attribution to Jews that they cherished a misconception about their Messias. But their deeper idolatry of fashioning*

*of God in the image of the Egyptian, Persian and Roman
imperial rulers was retained. The Church gave unto God the
attributes which belonged exclusively to Caesar.*[7]

A False Kingdom

Christianity has not impacted the world as a transforming
leaven because we have tried to make God and Jesus powerful in
the worldly sense of domination. We forget that God's "power is at
its best in weakness" (2 Cor 12:9). God has chosen a wisdom
different from the wisdom of this world. "For God's foolishness is
wiser than human wisdom, and God's weakness is stronger than
human strength" (1 Cor 1:25). We reason that if Jesus reveals to us
God — and we already know that God is omnipotent, all-knowing,
absolute in power and glory — then Jesus must be a King of power
and glory.

Becoming Like A Little Child

Jesus insists, however, that only those who have the qualities
of a child receive the Kingdom of God (Mk 10:15; Lk 18:17). Jesus
demands of us a conversion of heart, becoming little and humble,
receptive to God's activity in our lives. Otherwise, the Kingdom
that is before our very eyes cannot be recognized by us. A child —
who in its "littleness" is utterly dependent on others — becomes
the model for those who wish to enter into God's Kingdom. It is not
only a physical poverty (which in itself is valueless); it is a psychic
and spiritual poverty that recognizes the absolute sovereignty of
God. "How happy are the poor in spirit; theirs is the kingdom of
heaven. . . ." (Mt 5:3).

Such an interior poverty is the development of the *anima*,
diffused awareness, the ability to be open and receptive to God's
inbreaking with new life. It is letting go and letting God be God. It
is the ability to wait for God to speak — and then to obey in

childlike surrender. It is to become emptied of self-centeredness and to be oriented toward the other. Only then can we discover God in His unbelievable outpoured love in each moment. "I live in a high and holy place, but I am also with the contrite and humbled spirit, to give the humbled spirit new life, to revive contrite hearts" (Is 57:15).

Mary, the mother of Jesus in her *Magnificat* proclaims God's love and mercy shown to the lowly and humble (Lk 1:52-53). God will comfort those who mourn. He will show mercy to the merciful. The pure of heart shall see Him. He will call the peacemakers His own children. The Kingdom of Heaven is given to those who suffer persecution on behalf of God. They are to rejoice and be glad, for a great reward will be given them (Mt 5:3-12; Lk 6:20-23).

A Metanoia

Jesus preached that we must break away from our self-absorption and turn totally to God. This repentance is a complete upheaval of one's "carnal" thinking of an eye for an eye and a tooth for a tooth. It is a gift that God gives to those who earnestly go out of self to seek Him among the despised and the lowly. This "conversion" is a "losing" of one's life, a turning away from the false ego, to surrender completely to God as the inner, directing force in one's life. The seed has to die to itself before it can bring forth new life a hundredfold (Jn 12:24-25).

It is a slow process whereby God becomes the revolving axis of our lives. It is an enlightenment that is given by God to those who open up as earth to receive the seed of His Word. It is a "knowing" that is beyond human knowledge. We studied the apophatic theology of the early Eastern Christian mystics in order to prepare for the knowledge of a crucified God that no human wisdom could ever comprehend, let alone accept as a style of life.

From The Fruit To The Tree

In approaching God through the humanity of Christ, we follow the example of the first apostles. They experienced Jesus' humanity in His fullness. Through the gift of the Holy Spirit, they were able to experience Him as the living, risen Jesus, now the Lord, given a name that is above all other names as the Father exalts Him in glory.

As we reflect upon Jesus' life and teachings, we are led to ask who He is who lived such a life. We know that Jesus is substantially one with the same substance of the Father, *homo-ousia*, as the Council of Nicea (325) defined Him, and that He possesses two complete natures, divine and human, but in one person. Above all, we know that God has chosen to reveal Himself to us through the humanity of Christ.

We reach the "insideness" of that humanity by seeing the "ortho-praxis," the right living reflected in Jesus' life and teachings. His humanity is the only way we can come to know what God is like. If we begin with a complete idea of what God must be like, we strip the Incarnation of its power of "manifesting" the divine in and through the material world of Christ's humanity.

Jesus continually exhorted His disciples to bring forth fruit which alone would show that they had been regenerated by His Spirit to truly be children of God, participators in His divine nature (2 P 1:4). Jesus knew that His whole mission in life was to serve the Father's will, to reflect the Father's outpouring love in every decision and action. As He met the emptying love of His Father in each moment of His earthly life, Jesus knew that His service on behalf of God's people was to be pushed to such self-forgetting that He would make a free gift of Himself for the human race. He, the Good Shepherd, would lay down His life for all humanity. Thus He would become the concrete image and likeness of the Father.

No Greater Love
Than To Die For A Friend

Jesus' dying for others would be a totally free act of love on behalf of all who would believe in His outpoured, free gift of Himself. He would not be caught as a victim of religious or political intrigues. Nor did He see the Father decreeing all the details of His death. Daily as He grew in wisdom and knowledge and grace before God and men (Lk 2:52), Jesus experienced the *kenosis* or self-emptying love of His Father, breaking down all self-restraints and passionately pouring the fullness of divinity into His Son (Col 2:9). This self-emptying love begets a similar love in the heart of Jesus who lives for others as the Father lives for the Son. "As the Father has loved me, so I love you" (Jn 15:9).

Let us begin to study the kenotic Christ who reveals to us a God who empties Himself for each of us in perfect compassion and active concern for our complete happiness and fulfillment. We have spoken about a "new vision" in which God is revealed to us through the exploding universe that boggles our human minds. Here we need to see in faith and humility that the greatest power in the universe, the true power of God, is the power of self-emptying love, perfectly revealed to us by the crucified Jesus on the cross.

He Emptied Himself

There have always been mystics, preachers, writers and theologians who have seen the death of Jesus on the cross as the key revelation of the Incarnate Word of God. Yet so many of them had difficulties in properly expressing this "kenotic" revelation of God.[8]   This is especially true of the 19th century German theologian, Gottfried Thomasius.

Thomasius insisted, in commenting on the Incarnation and especially the text of Philippians 2:6-11, that the eternal Logos, in His *kenosis* or emptying, laid aside the relational attributes of omnipotence, omniscience and omnipresence. These attributes are not, he thought, essential to God Himself, but are expressive of a relationship God has entered into freely and from which He can withdraw.[9]

These "kenotic" theologians failed to show that God's transcendence is His very immanence. Highlighting God's immutability and transcendence, they were unable to show that in Christ's *kenosis* (or self-emptying of His divinity in taking upon Himself our humanity) "parts" of God's divinity were not surrendered.

Karl Barth, among the modern "kenoticists," shows that Christ's *kenosis* is not a loss at all in God's divinity, but is a sign of awesome transcendence to go beyond Himself to relate to mankind by actually becoming an individual man. The *kenosis* of Christ is the highest affirmation and revelation of God's humble transcendence, as love outpoured so completely that God, as Trinity, becomes immanently present to all human beings by becoming one of them. He writes:

> *The way of the Son of God into the far country, i.e., into the lowliness of creaturely being, of being as man, into unity and solidarity with sinful and therefore perishing humanity, the way of His incarnation is as such the activation, the demonstration, the revelation of His divine Sonship.*[10]

Humanity Reveals Divinity

Piet Schoonenberg in his exegesis of Ph 2:6-11 stresses that what Jesus "gives up" is the habitual attitude that most people have of God as all-powerful, immutable and, therefore, unrelated to the human situation. Jesus chooses the role of a suffering servant through His self-emptying of any worldly power and His rejection of all lust and abuse of any independent power. He wishes in His human actions to reveal the Father and Himself as love by self-emptying. The more He gives Himself for people, the more fully does He manifest what God is truly like; outpoured love toward us.[11]

A kenotic Christology has as its fundamental basis the question of who and what God is in relation to His created world, especially to us human beings. Does God love His material creation (Jn 3:16)? Is the Incarnation a step down for God — or is it the way God reveals Himself to us, not as a lesser deity, but in His likeness as Love?

Modern theologians, as K. Rahner, H. Kung, W. Pannenberg, J. Moltmann and D. Bonhoeffer, point out that God's relationship to His creatures is not an imperfect but a glorious revelation of God as suffering love. Many insist that the concept of the suffering, emptying Jesus as a perfect imaging of God's inner nature demands a grounding within the mystery of God as Trinity.[12]

Trinitarian Relationships

If the *kenosis* of Christ is not a diminishing of the divine nature but a positive, perfect expression of it, then it is of the essence of God as love and, therefore, God as Trinity. The Greek Fathers used the word *ek-stasis*, ecstasy or going beyond one's self in self-giving toward the other, thus finding one's true personhood in that relationship.

The Christian doctrine of the Trinity did not evolve out of Greek metaphysics but from the experience of God's kenotic love in the crucified and risen Christ. The early Christians saw that God's very nature was to be in loving, kenotic relationship within the Godhead.

In the Trinity the Father, Son and Holy Spirit essentially empty themselves in loving sacrifice toward each other. Karl Rahner gives us a basic principle when he declares that the relationships of the Trinity within the community between Father and Son in the same Spirit of love are the same relationships of the Trinity outward toward the created world.[13]   Creation and Incarnation, he holds, are understandable only in terms of their relation to the procession of the Word within the Godhead.

Gabriel Marcel insists that in any person-to-person love relationship — through intimate presence that means total availability, mutuality and self-gifting to the other — the *I* is the child of the *We*. We cannot conceive the three Persons within the Trinity in static terms. Personhood is a process of *becoming* through freely positing oneself as a gift in love to the other. Such an interchange not only brings about a unity but also a differentiation and a uniqueness of each person involved.

The Father does not exist independent of the Son, nor the Son independent of the Father, nor the Spirit independent of both the Father and the Son. There can be no Father but as revealed in the light of His loving relationships to the Son and Spirit. There can be no Son existing within the Trinity independent of His essential relationship to the Father who begets Him eternally in and through His Spirit of love. Such a begetting and being begotten cannot be possible except as manifest through the Spirit that is the hidden, kenotic self-emptying Love personified, uniting the Father and the Son, and yet at the same time bringing about the uniqueness of each Person in His "otherness."

Such implosive love toward the Other within the Trinity bursts out in a kenotic self-emptying through which both the Godhead and the three unique Persons seek to be one and many in relationship to the otherness of creation.[14]   If love is essentially self-giving on behalf of the other, then at the heart of God's Triune community is *kenosis*, a constant self-emptying movement of love in order to be "other-centered." We see that the paradox that Jesus taught and lived is found at the heart of the Trinity itself. Emptying through love for another is really an in-filling; poverty of spirit is true richness; death to self-centeredness is really new life in resurrection and glory. True perfection consists not in holding on to one's being, but in the weakness of always giving oneself away on behalf of the other, of saying: "I cannot be myself without you!"

God's Mutability

We have already pointed out in earlier chapters how St. Thomas Aquinas taught that God is immutable, unchanging, perfect and independent in His complete transcendence — and therefore that He cannot have a *real* relationship with the material world, including us human beings. It is only we who can truly relate to God because we depend upon Him.[15]   But if the biblical God in His revelation through actions among His people is shown to be a God of pathos,[16]   then He must be in real and dynamic relationships. If the intimate relationships within the Trinity are the same as the relationships of the triune God toward us, then we must acknowledge that God truly relates to us in the self-emptying gift of Himself to us in Jesus Christ.

Thus the distinction made by Scripture, the Greek Fathers and the modern process-theologians (following Whitehead's insights) must be held for a valid Christianity. God in His essence is perfect, immutable and independent of any outside agent. In His "primordial nature," God contains an infinity of possibilities of relationships to innumerable possible outside "others" including the otherness of Jesus Christ.

God is di-polar. He is transcendent and absolute subsistence in Himself, yet He is supremely *relative*. He gives created beings their "otherness," yet He also wants to receive a return of love from them. God is eternal, but also active and receptive in creation and redemption. He is impassible, but also "passible." He is the "inside," immanent ground of all beings, but is not dependent upon creatures to complete Himself.

God's eternal, perfect nature as self-emptying love within the Trinity freely calls out for a complementary self-giving to the created world in which He becomes the "insideness" of its very being. Pseudo-Dionysius calls this God's *going out* of Himself in creation and redemption (in Greek, *proodos*) in order freely to create so as to give and share His Triune community with His human creatures. It is important to always keep in mind that God freely chooses to limit Himself to bring "others" into being in time and space. He freely limits Himself to wait upon our free response.

A Suffering God

God freely chooses to share His loving being with rational creatures by surrendering His self-sufficiency and independence and by waiting upon others in whom He resides as their source of existence. He never loses His transcendence and perfection as Supreme Being by consenting to be the immanent source of all created reality. "In Him we live and move and have our being" (Ac 17:28). He now becomes an actualized possibility — other than God in His essence. He is now present and self-giving as the ground of being of each of His creatures.

God respects our freedom and does not coerce us. He offers His self-gift to "entice" or "allure" us to return His gift of love. This kenotic mutability in His self-communication does not lessen His perfection, nor can such self-limitation in a changing world affected by our free choices be separated from His immutable essence.

Karl Rahner shows that God's possibility of being in relationship to us is not an imperfection, but rather is a manifestation of the greatest of His perfections:

> *This perfection would be less perfect if he could not become less than he is. . . . The absolute, or, more correctly, the absolute One in the pure freedom of His infinite unrelatedness, while he always preserves, possesses the possibility of himself becoming the other, the finite.* [17]

God is changed and affected, not in His essence, but in and through His relationships with His creatures. Such possibility must mean that God remains completely "other" and independent of all His creatures, yet He is totally present and self-giving of Himself as the ground of being of His creatures and the ultimate Source of their fulfillment and happiness.

We are worthwhile in God's eyes. He waits for our loving response. He is affected by our decisions. We may be sinful, "black but lovely," as the Song of Songs describes the already and the not yet of our transformation by cooperating with God's self-gift (Sg 1:5). The secret of our transformation — and our affecting the world by our own creativity in oneness with the infinite creativity of God — is that we experience God's personal, loving activity in the events of our daily lives. This is why Jesus Christ alone is the Way that leads us to God as kenotic love. Through His resurrectional presence within both us and the material world, we can "co-create" this world. We can bring it into a fullness that will affect God by bringing Him a perfection that He would not have experienced without creation and the redemptive order through the Incarnation. P. Hodgson describes what a completed world brings to God:

> *God will not be the same God upon the consummation of all things and their return to the Father as he was prior to the act of creation. In this sense he will have 'become' something 'other' and will have experienced something 'more' than was the case when God was God for himself alone.*[18]

Love Unto Death

In Christ's suffering for us, especially dying on the cross, we have an image of how great is God's desire to associate with our sufferings. Jesus, in His compassion and active love in self-giving, enters into the very depths of our sin and death. He becomes our "fellow-sufferer" and chooses humanly to be like God. Jesus' Incarnation is the most perfect way of imaging the eternal love of the Father for us. We cannot know the inner being of the incomprehensible God except through the revelation of the Son. In Him as involved, suffering love, freely given for us, we have the perfect expression in human language of the very being of God.

Jesus' lifetime of suffering for us is climaxed in the most powerful *kenosis* of His crucifixion. There, He screamed out: "My God, my God, why have you deserted me?" (Mk 15:34). The emptying of the suffering servant of Yahweh reaches its peak on Calvary. God is being manifested for each of us as Love, perfect in His self-surrender. "A man can have no greater love than to lay down his life for his friends" (Jn 15:13). We might also add: "Nor can God." God reaches the peak of speaking His Word. He can be no more present as Love than in His Image, Jesus Christ, poured out on the cross, even to the last drop of blood, made sin, rejected and outcast to become one with us in our brokenness.

A Suffering Father

Can we not also accept the Father as a suffering servant on our behalf? We must always avoid the 3rd-4th century heresy called "Patripassianism," that taught that the Father also underwent the passion in the mode of Jesus' suffering body. But how can the Father remain unmoved? Love cannot ignore the sufferings of the one loved. The Father must be in His Word. The Image must reflect "honestly" the One imaged. "Who sees me sees the Father," Jesus said (Jn 14:9).

Gerald Vann, O.P. gives us an insight as to how God can suffer with and for us:

> But in the life of God there are no events; God has no history.
> Eternity is not an endless line running parallel with the line
> of time; it is a point; and what to us is past or future is as

*much present to eternity as is the actual moment we are now
living. . . . Thus the very immutability of God is not a
denial of his involvement in the sorrows of these present
times, but a triumphant vindication of it. Of the human body
of Christ you can say that first it suffered, and then it was
glorified and made glad; but throughout that temporal
sequence the Godhead remains unchanged and unchanged
precisely in its knowledge and willing of, and its will to share
in, that which Christ on the Cross took to himself and made
his own and in his glorification turned into glory.*[19]

For Me He Dies

We can give an intellectual assent to the historical fact that
Jesus lived and died as a suffering servant. We can believe He is the
image of God. But unless we "experience" the reality of God
emptying Himself through His incarnate Word out of love for each
of us, it is as if God and His active love do not exist. There must be
a dialogue of love. The Father is always speaking His Word to us.
Jesus is always loving us unto death. He is now present in our lives
with that same dynamic, eternal love which He had when He died
to serve us. In prayer we must experience what St. Paul did: "The
life I now live in this body I live in faith: faith in the Son of God who
loved me and who sacrificed himself for my sake" (Gal 2:20). In
the context of our daily lives we dialogue with God's revealing
Word as emptying love. This daily experience leads us into the
awesome presence of the Heavenly Father as perfect holiness,
beauty and love. We realize that we are *now* being loved by our
infinitely loving Father through His emptying suffering servant,
Jesus Christ.

Such a healing of our loneliness and self-absorption begins to
transform our lives into ones of service to others. We live by the
exhortation of St. Paul: ". . . and the reason he died for all was so

that living men should live no longer for themselves, but for him
who died and was raised to life for them'' (2 Cor 5:15).

Living For Others

Th s knowledge and power come from God Himself, a source
beyond anything we can reason to, or effect by our own power.
Only in prayer can we experience God's Word speaking to us,
quietly and deeply, of His presence as suffering love. Jesus sheds
His blocd and we are redeemed by it. But this is a process in
dialogue through faith, hope and love, discovered in prayer which
the hidden power of God's love, the Holy Spirit, gives us.

We come to see that redemption and creation are not static,
objective, moments of the past. Each day in prayer, we can
discover afresh that the Father, Son and Spirit live in serving love.
Such love is always the eternal, unchanging, unconditional self-
giving of God to us in His uncreated energies of love. Yet such love
is ever being unveiled in new and exciting ways. Every human
situation can work unto good (Rm 8:28) if we have ''eyes'' to see
God, self-giving in the matter at hand. Christ still washes our feet;
He willingly bears the cross; He dies for us as a sign of His
passionate love for each of us.

Love begets love. Our awareness of God's personalized self-
giving to us in Jesus Christ who lives within us, leading us always
into the heart of the Trinity, impels us to live lives of selfless
charity. God is calling us to let His serving Word go among our
neighbors, localizing His loving presence through you and me.

Christ Is My Neighbor

When God's kenotic love overcomes us, we realize that
everyone is our neighbor. But it is more than this. God's alluring
presence to draw us into a similar self-emptying love is discovered
in our neighbor. We not only love all people with God's universal

and unconditional love, but we are really loving God who is immanently present in all created beings.

Now we can understand what Jesus teaches in His discourse about the final judgment:

> *"Come, blessed of my Father, take possession of the king-dom prepared for you from the foundation of the world. For I was hungry and you gave me food; I was thirsty and you gave me drink; I was a stranger and you made me welcome; naked and you clothed me; sick and you visited me; in prison and you came to see me." Then the virtuous will say to him in reply, "Lord, when did we see you hungry and feed you; or thirsty and give you drink? When did we see you a stranger and make you welcome; naked and clothe you; sick or in prison and go to see you?" And the King will answer, "I tell you solemnly, in so far as you did this to one of the least of these brothers of mine, you did it to me"* (Mt 25:34-40).

To look on the face of a son or daughter of God is to see a holy face. Our neighbors may not realize how beautiful they are in God's passionate love for them individually. In their loneliness, fears and anxieties they may be unaware of God's emptying love from within them. But you and I are called by faith to go beyond the externals. God's Spirit allows us to enter by loving service into the core of our neighbor's being where God abides as compassionate and co-suffering community of *I-Thou* in the Trinity. There we touch God and neighbor, a unity in diversity. God one with His suffering human child.

Our neighbor is the face of Christ Himself. It may be defaced. Yet we are called to the great dignity of restoring with God's involving, uncreated energies of love the fullness of that beauty. Jesus, the suffering servant of God, lives in us, loves in us and wishes to serve His broken brothers and sisters through us. By God's presence as self-emptying love in Jesus Christ, we are empowered to beget God's actualized presence in the neighbor whom we serve and in the world we are called by God to co-create with Him.

By dying to ourselves, we live for others and find our true selves in them. In living for others, we please God and affect Him by allowing Him to know Himself in new ways as "other" in the otherness of the neighbor. Loving, humble service to any and all of our brothers and sisters — especially to the least and the smallest, the oppressed and the fearful, the lonely and the depraved — is the sign that Jesus is Lord and is redeeming us, freeing us to become the focus of God's Word. He is revealing a Father who also is a suffering servant as He brings us and creation into a oneness with Jesus Christ, the one who is one with God and is still the otherness of creation that thrills the heart of God, the Lover of mankind.

ENDNOTES

1 Friedrich Nietzsche: "Thus Spake Zarathustra," in: *The Philosophy of Nietzsche* (N.Y.: Modern Library, n.d.) p. LXXII.

2 F. Nietzsche: *The Birth of Tragedy and the Genealogy of Morals* (Garden City, N.Y.: Doubleday 1965), pp. 149-188.

3 Abraham Joshua Heschel: *The Prophets* (N.Y.: Harper & Row, 1971), Vol. 2; Ch. 1, passim.

4 On the biblical concept of God as vulnerable, cf.: Burton Z. Cooper: *The Idea of God* (The Hague: M. Nyhoff, 1974), p. 5.

5 Pastoral Constitution, "Gaudium et Spes," in Walter Abbott: *Documents of Vatican II* (N.Y.: America Press, 1966), p. 220.

6 Gregory Baum: *Man Becoming* (N.Y.: Herder & Herder, 1970), p. 37.

7 Alfred North Whitehead: *Process and Reality* (.N.Y.: Macmillan, 1929), pp. 519-520.

8 For a review of the "kenotic theologians" of the 19th and 20th centuries, see the work of Lucien J. Richard, OMI: *A Kenotic Christology* (Lanham, MD: Univ. Press of America, 1982).

9 Ibid., p. 159

10 Karl Barth: *Church Dogmatics*; tr. by G.W. Bromiley (Edinburgh, 1956) Vol. IV, Part I, p. 211. C. D. Dawe: *The Form of a Servant* (Philadelphia: Fortress, 1964), pp. 160-176.

11 Piet Schoonenberg, S.J.: "The Kenosis or Self-Emptying of Christ," *Concilium* Vol. I, 2, (1966), pp. 47-66 passim.

12 Cf.: C. Duquoc: *Christologie, L'Homme Jesus* (Paris: Desclée, 1968) Vol. I, pp. 329-336; Jurgen Moltmann: *The Crucified God* (London: SCM Press, Ltd., 1974), p. 206, 256; Karl Rahner: "Trinity," in: *Encyclopedia of Theology* (N.Y.: Seabury Press,

1965), pp. 1758-1762; also: *Dictionary of Theology* (N.Y.: Seabury, 1965), p. 115; Hans Urs von Balthasar: *Le Mystere Pascal*, Coll. *Mysterium Salutis* (Paris: Aubier, 1972), pp. 13-275.

13 Karl Rahner: *Dictionary of Theology*, p. 115.

14 For an extensive discussion of "darkness" or a realizable perfection of God within the Trinity and in relationships to God's creatures see: E.R. Baltazar: *The Dark Center* (N.Y.: Paulist, 1974).

15 St. Thomas: *Summa Theologiae*; Prima Pars, 13, 7 ad 4.

16 On the pathos of God, cf.: Robert Wild: *Who I will be — Is There Joy and Suffering in God?* (Denville, N.J.: Dimension Books, 1976); J. Moltmann: *The Crucified God*, pp. 271-276; A.J. Heschel: *The Prophets*, Vol. 2, Ch. 1: "The Theology of Pathos."

17 Karl Rahner: *Foundations of Christian Faith* (N.Y.: Seabury, 1978), p. 222.

18 P. Hodgson: *Jesus — Word and Presence. An Essay in Christology* (Philadelphia: Fortress Press, 1971), p. 128.

19 Gerald Vann, O.P.: *The Pain of Christ and the Sorrow of God* (London: Blackfriars, 1947) pp. 67-69.

CHAPTER

8

Called To Freedom

We have been reflecting on God's exploding love toward us. His uncreated energies bombard us at every instant. We are surrounded and penetrated by God's personalized self-giving as a loving community of Persons, Father, Son and Holy Spirit. Our God is not a static, totally independent deity. God is ever in loving, active, energetic relationships with us and all creation. Although God is completely transcendent in His unique self-subsistent Being, we turn to our Christian faith to discover that His very transcendence is the basis of His immanent presence as creator and preserver of all creatures.

In our final chapter we wish to explore the unique quality that separates us from other creatures and gives us a sharing in God's own nature (2 P 1:4). We are called to a great dignity. Through our human freedom, we can see how we are to respond to the self-emptying love of God for us.

How does God call us without forcing our response? If God is involved in our lives and we are co-creators of this world with Him, how can God be both eternal and temporal? Is there potentiality in God that becomes actualized by our free response? Does God eagerly await, want and somehow need our "yes" response?

Human Dignity

As we seek love, we also seek freedom. Love and freedom are not identical, but each needs the other as its complement. God, who is love (1 Jn 4:8), is also the perfection of freedom. We cannot comprehend what true love and freedom should mean in our lives unless we understand how God is both love and freedom. The spark we are that emanates out of the flaming heart of God can be known only from its Source.

We are created by God in His own image and likeness, to share in His love and freedom. The trinitarian community of loving, free Persons bursts out in creative freedom to "other" themselves in the otherness of creation. God freely wishes to bestow upon us a sharing in self-creation and self-transcendence. This is a sharing in God's own love, His Spirit. The Spirit's freedom is at the essence of God's nature.

We are the overflow of God's fullness of love and freedom. In God's utter selflessness because He is All, His goodness created us. Better yet, God is continually creating us. But in making us in His image, He waits for our free response in loving service to Himself and our neighbor. Emil Brunner beautifully describes this fundamental relationship to the Father through His creative Word in the freedom of the Spirit:

> *God creates man in such a way that in this very creation man is summoned to receive the Word actively, that is, he is called to listen, to understand, and to believe. God creates man's being in such a way that man knows that he is determined and conditioned by God, and in this fact is truly human. The being of man as an "I" is being from and in the Divine "Thou," or, more exactly, from and in the Divine Word, whose claim "calls" man's being into existence. . . . The characteristic imprint of man, however, only develops on the basis of Divine determination, as an answer to a call,*

by means of a decision. The necessity for decision, an obligation which he can never evade, is the distinguishing feature of man . . . it is the being created by God to stand "over-against" Him, who can reply to God, and who in this answer alone fulfills or destroys the purpose of God's creation.[1]

Our dignity through God's ongoing creative, loving energies consists in being able to know God's love and to freely respond to His allurements of love. God is constantly drawing us to freely say "yes" to His invitation, so that we can be refashioned in His true image, His divine Son. St. Paul puts it succinctly: "You have put on the new man, that is being renewed unto knowledge after the image of Him that created him" (Col 3:10).

The whole world is charged with God's energizing power and love. He freely creates the world as a gift to us. We stand in this universe as God's masterpiece. He entrusts to us the richness of the created world, "to cultivate and take care of it" (Gn 2:15). We are created and endowed with body, soul and spirit relationships to God and the rest of the created world. God invites us to receive His gift of love and to freely decide to return that love by giving of ourselves to God and neighbor in free love. We also have the horrendous power, as history so often shows, to refuse God's gifts.

Modern Images Of The Human Person

The lack of freedom and love in our lives makes us see ourselves and others in such a way that we remain aloof, detached, independent of them, entirely self-centered. As we form our own self-image, so we behave toward God and other people.

The great writers and philosophers have fashioned for us a *pantheon* of human models for our guidance. The mass media have also created a variety of images of the human person.[2] Darwin showed that man is "naturally" related to the whole animal world, while Marx showed that man is essentially social by nature and would eventually end all class societies. But Arthur Koestler in *Darkness at Noon*[3]   shows us the disaster of sacrificing the individual for an abstract cause. Henri Bergson[4]   and Teilhard de Chardin[5]   present us with man in the process of becoming human in the matrix of a creative dynamism of interacting relationships in love.

We are mystics underneath our struggling, sinful, failing human nature, according to T.S. Eliot and George Bernanos. Sigmund Freud and Carl Jung give us the psychological man, while Erich Fromm thinks that we are basically pragmatic.

Reacting against idealistic abstractions, existential philosophers like Friedrich Nietzsche, Jean-Paul Sartre, Soren Kierkegaard, Paul Tillich, Albert Camus and Martin Buber depict modern man and woman as struggling for meaning in their everyday life with its share of absurdity and confusion.

Modern tabloids, novels, TV programs, movies, songs and advertisements fashion a great variety of images of man and woman — but self-centeredness and confusion seem to be the key characteristics.

Born To Be Free

We moderns sit in the narrowness of our shrunken world, pathetically seeking to return to the freedom God originally meant us to enjoy. Our destiny is to participate in God's own nature (2 P 1:4). The beauty and nobility of the human person is described by the Psalmist:

> *Ah, what is man that you should spare a thought for him, the son of man that you should care for him? Yet you have made him little less than a god, you have crowned him with glory and splendor, made him lord over the work of your hands, set all things under his feet (Ps 8:5-7).*

We are made by God in an ongoing process to know His love and to freely respond by deciding to obey His will. We do that when we live and act always out of love for Himself and for all others. We are not meant to sacrifice true freedom by acting slavishly or out of selfishness. God's love permeates the universe with His uncreated energies of creative power. He invites us through His Spirit of love to become co-creators of this magnificent universe.

To be human means to become ever more free in each choice made out of love as we respond to God's call to be free. Our human dignity consists in affirming our true selfhood through self-giving in loving service to others. God calls us into communion with His own divine life, but on terms of our human freedom and responsiveness. God limits His omnipotence to express and communicate His loving gift of Himself to us through His constant, creative actions. He never coerces us but gently persuades us by "alluring" acts of suffering love.

Brokenness And Servitude

But when we look at the history of the human race and in particular our own personal history, we find that we are "yo-yo" people. We go up and down on a string, manipulated by forces within us and around us, from the past and from the present. We are shadows of what we could be, of what God wants us to become by His grace.

We are locked inside ourselves. We are sick, anemic, afraid, cut off from God and neighbor. We sense at every turn a keen frustration, a dim awareness that we were meant by God to be "whole" people. Instead, we feel our disintegration. Our body wars against our soul; our soul slashes out at our inner spirit.

We try to give others the impression that we are happy and healthy. But we know that we are lonely, that we have an inner force that drives us away from love to seek our sick refuge in a false independence. What brokenness we discover deep in our psyche! What fears cruelly assail us day and night! Doubts, anger, depression, hatred and resentment seethe within us like a gigantic, smoldering volcano that needs the slightest tremor to pour forth its molten lava.

St. Paul well understood this inner force that kept him a slave to sin:

> *In fact, this seems to be the rule, that every single time I want to do good it is something evil that comes to hand. In my inmost self I dearly love God's Law, but I can see that my body follows a different law that battles against the law which my reason dictates. This is what makes me a prisoner of that law of sin which lives inside my body. What a wretched man I am! Who will rescue me from this body doomed to death? Thanks be to God through Jesus Christ our Lord! (Rm 7:18-24).*

A World Groaning In Travail

Not only do we experience our own individual servitude and lack of freedom to love, but we find that we have been led into this bondage through the actions and reactions of countless persons and events and institutions. This is what St. Paul calls "the sin of the world." Our darkness is a part of the world's darkness, our self-centeredness a part of the world's self-centeredness. It is ours simply by being part of the human race. We share also in the brokenness and "worldliness" found in the Body of Christ, the Church. This is the servitude of the human race that God wants to redeem.

You and I have become what we are and what we will be through our actions upon and reactions to other individuals. Our parents, friends, teachers, wife, husband, children, enemies and even "indifferent" acquaintances have helped to make us what we are by their attitudes, acts and even omissions — by their lack of freedom their lack of love.

Freedom In A Loving Community

Genuine freedom is born out of true love. This means that true love comes out of an *I-Thou* in a *We* community of love. But the first step toward true freedom is to hear God's constant call to love. Wherever people, alone or in groups, show Christ's love in their loving service and self-giving to others, that call is being heard.

The first stage in answering this call is to realize that we are not free and that we are in need of a conversion. This is the Gospel *metanoia* which in Greek means literally to have an overhauling of all our perceptions of ourselves, of God, of our neighbors, of this world. St. Paul calls this liberation from the "flesh." This is not the renunciation of our basic, God-given instincts and passions. *Flesh* for St. Paul and the other New Testament writers refers to the slavery of self-love and the inability to love anyone else. It flows out of the desire for things as tokens of power and independence, out of selfishness, vanity and lack of love.

St. Paul describes this *metanoia*:

> In particular, I want to urge you in the name of the Lord, not
> to go on living the aimless kind of life that pagans live.
> Intellectually they are in the dark, and they are estranged
> from the life of God, without knowledge because they have
> shut their hearts to it. Their sense of right and wrong once
> dulled, they have abandoned themselves to sensuality and
> eagerly pursued a career of indecency of every kind. Now
> that is hardly the way you have learnt from Christ, unless
> you failed to hear him properly when you were taught what
> the truth is in Jesus. You must give up your old way of life;
> you must put aside your old self, which gets corrupted by

following illusory desires. Your mind must be renewed by a
spiritual revolution so that you can put on the new self that
has been created in God's way, in the goodness and holiness
of the truth (Ep 4:17-24).

St. Paul insists on this: "For you were called to freedom"
(Gal 5:13). We are not born free. But God calls all His children to
respond to His call and enter into the process of continued growth in
freedom and in love for each other and for God. We are called not
to "feel" saved, but to experience an "absolute feeling of freedom" in communion with the free God.[6]   The German poet
Schiller saw that "man is free and he was born in chains." Our
chains drop when we respond to God's call to liberation. Liberation
is the process by which we cooperate with God's grace to be
delivered from the forces that keep us bound. It is the necessary
step to attaining true freedom.

Liberation sets us on the path to become truly "human." But
the added step that knows no end of growth is our free mutual love
toward others in self-sacrificing actions on their behalf. We become true children of God when, with His grace, we can live for
others and no longer for ourselves.

Two roads confront us in life's decisions. One is to choose out
of the "flesh," out of selfishness or self-love — as St. Maximus
the Confessor in the 7th century called it, *philautia,* love of oneself. The other is to move into true freedom. This is a true conversion in which we regard others as persons, worthy of our respect,
born as we are in the likeness of God Himself. No longer are others
mere objects. In some way they are an extension of ourselves, vital
parts of the Body of Christ of which we also are parts. We cannot
now live without others, or be indifferent to them, or look down in
judgment upon them.

Experiencing True Love

Freedom and love cannot exist without each other. All of us have experienced a freeing love received from others, hopefully beginning with our parents and relatives. But the peak of true love is found in the Trinity which is love itself.

God calls us to freedom by the outpouring of His passionate love for each one of us. It is only through love experienced that we become freed from isolation and self-centeredness, in order to give this godly love to others in community. It is God's love that heals. This love has become incarnated for us in Jesus of Nazareth. God's Word has been definitively spoken to us in His person, especially in His suffering and crucifixion. By His wounds we are healed of our wounds. By His freeing love we are set free to love others. Jesus becomes a "slave" for us, dying for us, in order to free us and allow us to live in loving service for every person we meet.

True freedom is found in the decision to live as God lives, shown by the Word Incarnate, Jesus Christ. Nicholas Berdyaev, the twentieth century Russian philosopher, describes true freedom as a victory in the area of the spiritual world:

> . . . *Freedom must be loving and love must be free. It is only the gathering together of freedom, truth and love which realizes personality, free and creative personality. Man passes from slavery to freedom, from a state of disintegration to a condition of completeness, from impersonality to personality, from passivity to creativeness, that is to say, he passes over to spirituality.*[7]

Yet how reluctantly we move toward freedom and away from self-centeredness! We must move toward freed love. This is "living in the heart," in the deeper recesses of our consciousness, informed by grace through the Spirit's infusion of faith, hope and love. Freedom is ultimately a move toward a loving gift of oneself to another, and this always necessitates a real *dying* process. It is a moving away from outside values that formerly determined our choices.

Dr. Carl Rogers, from a modern psychological viewpoint, describes this freedom:

> *Freedom to be oneself is a frighteningly responsible freedom, and an individual moves toward it cautiously, fearfully, and with almost no confidence at first. . . . They are in flux, and seem more content to continue in this flowing current.*[8]

We must open ourselves to God's freeing love as revealed through His incarnate Son, Jesus Christ. We find the qualities of His love to be situated within the immanent, loving, free actions of self-giving in the Trinity. The first characteristic of both divine and human freedom (since we share in God's image) is on the level of being: God is self-creative. God is revealed to us by Christ as a community of three Persons who are self-caused, self-determined, thus self-creating.

The Father freely determines to pour out the fullness of being into the Son (Col 2:9). He is not coerced by the Son or the Holy Spirit. The Son freely determines to return the gift of Himself to the Father through the Holy Spirit. We can say, quoting the phrase of Dr. Bernard M. Loomer: "The self is its decision. The self as its decision is what it makes of what it has been given to work with. . . ."[9]

Unlike the Trinity, we have a past and a present which affect our future possibilities. Within the limits of our past, we have the self-creative freedom to make decisions out of responsive love toward ourselves, God, our neighbor and the world.

We are not the sum of our past and our limitations. As Shakespeare writes — we can be masters sometimes, of our fate. God acts in our actions. But the awesome mystery of our human freedom lies in our *solitariness*. God in His humility and creative love-actions comes close to us and, as it were, stops at the periphery of our unique being to invite us to act out of love for Him and His creatures. Our terrifying "aloneness" cannot be invaded, not ever by God. In such self-creation and freedom we stand alone! Here we are the most *alone* but also the most *free* — to determine our fate to live by love for others or to live for ourselves.

Self-Transcendence

True freedom extends self-creation into its complementary quality of self-transcendence. It highlights even more our creation according to God's image and likeness. It is God's Spirit of love urging us to stretch beyond imposed limitations from the past and the present. The Spirit calls us to yearn, to burn, to become more transcendent, more beautiful, more unified and yet more uniquely individuated than before.

It is a movement *beyond* all limitations. It is the pain we experience in our union with God in prayer — or with our loved ones in love — that is never satisfied with the "already" but passionately desires the "not yet." This ability to soar to ever greater heights can be called our *spirit*.

Freedom And Evil

We have all been made for love and freedom. We are called, in each decision, to become our true self by reaching out to God in selfless love for others. To become freer and hence happier and more fulfilled, we must move beyond our "carnal" or exterior selves to respond and co-create with God our true or inner person.

Dr. Carl Rogers describes those people who find greater and greater freedom through self-transcendence:

> *They move toward being persons who accept and even enjoy their own feelings, who value and trust the deeper layers of their nature, who find strength in being their own unique-*

ness, who live by values they experience. This learning, this movement, enables them to live as more individuated, more creative, more responsive, and more responsible persons.[10]

What level of freedom have we attained in our daily choices? We stand dizzily on the heights of the universe, tempted as Jesus was in the desert. We can bow in loving surrender to our Father's majesty and tender love, or we can walk away into the darkness of self-centered love. We want desperately to live in freedom. Yet how we fear to let go of our control and power — which are illusory anyway — in order to "pass-over" in self-transcendence to live in faith, hope and love for God and others.

Feodor Dostoevsky in *The Brothers Karamazov* pinpoints our fundamental struggle in regard to God's call to freedom. In the "Legend of the Grand Inquisitor" he has the Grand Inquisitor say to Jesus (who has returned to 16th century Spain):

Instead of taking men's freedom from them, Thou didst make it greater than ever! Didst Thou forget that man prefers peace, and even death, to freedom of choice in the knowledge of good and evil? Nothing is more seductive for man than his freedom of conscience, but nothing is a greater cause of suffering. . . . Instead of taking possession of men's freedom, Thou didst increase it, and burdened the spiritual kingdom of mankind with its sufferings forever. Thou didst desire man's free love, that he should follow Thee freely, enticed and taken captive by Thee. In place of the rigid ancient law, man must hereafter with free heart decide for himself what is good and what is evil, having only Thy image before him as his guide. But didst Thou not know that he would at last reject even Thy image and Thy truth, if he is weighted down with the fearful burden of free choice?[11]

The problem of evil has always plagued mankind. Evil is very real. It is much more than a primitive attempt to explain the unknown. There are people — singly and in groups — who freely choose to live out of self-centeredness and not out of self-transcendent love. Often they choose to do evil, not with conscious malice, but in ignorance and blindness. They "miss the mark" of living in loving harmony within themselves and toward others and the world. They willingly prefer the "darkness" in order to escape the "light." They desperately avoid the pain of acting out of greater self-awareness and self-transcendence.

Dr. Scott Peck in *The Road Less Traveled* stresses the element of *laziness* behind so much of human evil:

> . . . evil is laziness carried to its ultimate, extraordinary extreme. As I have defined it, love is the antithesis of laziness. Ordinary laziness is a passive failure to love. . . . Truly evil people actively rather than passively avoid extending themselves. They will take any action in their power to protect their own laziness, to preserve the integrity of their sick self. Rather than nurturing others, they will actually destroy others in this cause. If necessary, they will even kill to escape the pain of their spiritual growth. . . . Ordinary laziness is nonlove; evil is antilove.[12]

Evil Unto Good

A.N. Whitehead, in pondering the problem of evil through our free choices, insists that God in His transcendence and "humility" stays with His children in their choices. When they have turned from God's "lure" of beauty and love to embrace self-centered motives, God meets them and seeks to "save" what can be saved in such a situation.

We have the chance to learn from the horrendous evils that have been committed in the past. We are also free not to profit from such experience. As individuals and as nations, we have the opportunity to choose either to respect the dignity of each person made uniquely beautiful by God, or to live in isolation and in selfishness.

We must always be ready to courageously encounter the forces of darkness and of light. We must enter within ourselves in the silence of honesty and poverty of spirit, to hear God speak His Word. Into the tomb of our inner darkness, the light of God's tender love bursts upon us. We weep tears of sorrow and repentance, of fright at our own *non-being*, as the rain of God's love falls upon the cracked, parched earth of our hearts. Seeds of new life begin to grow, to create a new and more beautiful world through love for each other and for God.

Freedom As Power

In every situation in which we close ourselves off from love, God's ever-constant love calls us to be reconciled to Him and our neighbor. Such reconciliation is an attempt on our part to actualize new choices of creativity.

Our freedom to co-create a better world with God and others is limited both by ourselves and by our social context. We simply cannot be everything we would wish to be, nor can this world in our lifetime become a perfect, utopian society.

Our freedom, therefore, will always be limited and crippled by the physical and psychological blocks imposed by the past, by the world around us, and by our own individual limitations. Many psychologists insist that we individually are using only 4½ to 5% of our potentiality. It is staggering to imagine, then, what potential lies within ourselves, within God's universe, within God Himself, to be actuated through our free cooperation!

Commitment To Freedom

The first stage of living in greater freedom is to humbly acccept the creaturely limitations of ourselves and the society in which we live. St. Paul lived in freedom within the context of the limiting "thorn in his flesh." We follow St. Paul's faith in the power of Christ to be his strength in his own weakness:

> So I shall be very happy to make my weaknesses my special boast so that the power of Christ may stay over me, and that is why I am quite content with my weaknesses, and with insults, hardships, persecutions, and the agonies I go through for Christ's sake. For it is when I am weak that I am strong (2 Cor 12:9-10).

We are truly free to the degree that we live in self-sacrificing love for God and neighbor. We are all self-creating persons who choose between good and evil. But the truly free person chooses what is loving, good, noble and beautiful. Such a person strives to choose always to be obedient in love to embrace God's will. That will for each of us is that we make every choice out of unselfish love.

We are free to the degree that we freely decide to live in love. But we become free only in order to love others, even unto persecutions and death itself in the cause of loving service.

The Eternal And The Temporal In God

The type of process-theology presented in this book seeks to break away from the mistaken idea that the eternal and unchanging Supreme Being could never have a "real" relationship with His "temporal" creatures.

We have already seen how God in His essence (Whitehead's "primordial" nature containing all possibilities) is truly independent of change, motion, time and matter. Yet divine revelation presents to us a powerful God, who freely out of perfect, selfless love decides to create us and call us to participate in His divine nature (2 P 1:4).

God's true power and perfection is to express and actuate new and enriching possibilities with our free, loving and creative cooperation. There is no lessening of God's perfection, omnipotence and eternity in His free choice to be involved in co-creating a more beautiful world with us. This evolving world will not only reveal God's beauty and perfection as love, but will add something to His perfection. He will be affected by our free, loving choices.

God is in the process of becoming the loving God of the universe in cooperation with our free choices. His essence consists in His free choice to work with us to make the world an adequate expression of His love. It is to move the world always toward new, enriching possibilities. In this sense, God is not at rest. He is vitally concerned with us — as He is affected by our free decisions, as He works to draw good out of each of our free choices.

We should not then contrast God in timeless eternity and creation in changing time. Daniel Day Williams expresses it well:

> *It is the contrast between the supremely creative temporal life of God and the fragmentary, limited creativity of the creatures. To love God, then, is to set the highest value on temporality as well as on eternality, for in this view temporality is a dimension of all value.* [13]

God loves each of us in our uniqueness. We are participators by God's free choice in the creative history of the world. To truly love God is to love the *Logos* in each person and in all creation. It is to work with God's creativity in time to bring joy to His heart through the fulfillment of His creation. God's relationship to His creation is not one of being an Oriental potentate, all powerful, before whom we grovel. The Kingdom of God is being brought about by God and us cooperating in loving creativity. God is an involved Creator in time; the temporality of this Kingdom will bring a new perfection to His eternality.

Daniel Day Williams (who follows the insights of Whitehead) beautifully describes God's and our loving involvement as always creative with a commitment toward self-giving in loving service:

> Love does not put everything at rest; it puts everything in motion. Love does not end all risk; it accepts every risk which is necessary for its work. Love does not resolve every conflict; it accepts conflict as the arena in which the work of love is to be done. Love does not neatly separate the good people from the bad, bestowing endless bliss on one, and endless torment on the other. Love seeks the reconciliation of every life so that it may share with all the others. If a man or culture is finally lost, it is not because love wills that lostness, but because we have condemned ourselves to separation and refuse reconciliation. We make our hells and we cling to them in our lovelessness.[14]

Grace As God's Luring Love

The doctrine of grace was traditionally taught in a static manner as a *quality*, a thing, created by God to supernaturally overcome the inherent incapacity of man's created, sin-infected nature to attain "eternal" life.

Now, we can see grace as primarily God's personalized, self-giving of His Triune community to us in each created moment. We can also see grace as God's "luring" actions to persuade us (but not to force us) to return His love by acting in love in union with His immanent presence within us and in all His creatures.[15]

God's Gift Of Himself

Grace for us must be seen as God's personalized presence to, and indwelling within, each human person. God's divine, energetic presence as love is always beckoning us to transcend the limits of our own self-possession. We do not seek, in prayer and good works, grace primarily as a gifted "thing," separable from God.

God personally is gifting us with His individuated, personalized gift, as Father, Son and Holy Spirit, in His love in each moment. Grace, therefore, is received in God's loving dialogue and activities with us in our world context. This is the sole reason for God's creation: to share His being through loving activity with us.

Possibilities For Prayer

Process theology offers us a more biblical approach to prayer, especially to petitional prayer to obtain favors from God. In the past it was hard to reconcile God's love with His omnipotence and omniscience. He knew in advance His static plans and all our free choices. Immanuel Kant, the German philosopher, felt that petitional prayer was absurd and presumptuous, an attempt to deflect God's wise plans to provide us with some momentary advantage, as though our will was greater than God's will.

True petitional prayer is not an attempt to ask God to change His mind. It is an attitude of total dependence upon God for everything:

> *It is all that is good, everything that is perfect, which is given us from above; it comes down from the Father of all light; with him there is no such thing as alteration, no shadow of a change. By his own choice he made us his children by the message of the truth so that we should be a sort of first-fruits of all that he had created (Jn 1:17-18).*

It is not God who needs to hear us express our needs. But we need such prayer, since it presupposes that everything comes to us from God. To be human is to recognize that we are not totally self-dependent. Prayer is not a call for help as much as it is our

acknowledgment that we receive everything from God and exist by
His grace.

David A. Fleming well describes petitional prayer from a
Whiteheadian process view:

> *In this view we can prevail upon God to "change" in a*
> *dynamic and creative sense: we freely contribute to the*
> *building of the universe by our acts, and God's concrete*
> *manner of caring for the universe will be influenced by our*
> *creative choices. The prayerful sharing of concerns in this*
> *view is surely not a way of asking the omnipotent to come*
> *down and supernaturally transform reality in accord with*
> *our wishes; rather it is a presentation of concerns regarding*
> *our own creative involvements, so that this concern may*
> *enter through God's consequent nature in the constant re-*
> *shaping of the initial aim and the order of relevance he*
> *provides to the universe in response to the free and creative*
> *actions of creatures. In this sense we can truly bring about a*
> *change in God's purposes for the universe, and petitionary*
> *prayer is a valid effort to bring this collaboration with God*
> *in creation more fully to our own consciousness and even*
> *into the responsive reality of his life.*[17]

God's uncreated energies of love invade our daily life at each
moment. The world, from God's viewpoint, is meant to move by
creative, loving activities into a greater unity. All creatures,
through the creative work of humanity cooperating with God, are
meant to become interrelated in a harmonious wholeness. Each
part has its proper place in the universe, its *logos* in oneness with
God's creative *Logos*. Each creature depends on and gives support
to all the others in one great body, all of which is being created in
and through God's Word with our human, free cooperation.

This wonderful, creating God is not only the powerful, transcendent Creator who stands above and outside of all His creation.
He is also the immanent force that lives inside of every creature

(Ac 17:28). He fills the heavens and the underworld. It is impossible to escape from His creative, sustaining Spirit (Ps 139:7).

God's Will Be Done

What, then, does doing God's will mean? Does He still have "plans" for our lives? We must move away from the childish view that placed all decisions about ourselves and the world upon God's holy will. It is, in Dietrich Bonhoeffer's phrase, "cheap grace" to do nothing in the face of human difficulties and passively wait for God to do something. We must respect God's sharing with us His own imageness and likeness. We have the ability to receive His love and freely return it by creative love.[18]   Our choices must always be made in prayer with discernment through faith, hope and love. However, all too many of us try to avoid our responsibilities.

God's will is manifested to us at all times by His Spirit of love, in which we live in every choice by transcendent, self-sacrificing love toward God and neighbor. He can "call" us to certain actions and life styles, but He does not coerce us to make one choice over another. God draws us; yet we are free to choose. God has many possibilities for us. He enters into our own choices to draw out possibilities we have never dreamed of — if we continue to dialogue in love with His providential care and "luring" love in each event.

There is plenty of room in our thought and prayer for God's particular providence, His loving "adaptation" to our free choices in order to bring out of each of them the best and greatest enrichment for us, for others and for His total creation.

Paschal Hope

As we pray and work in union with God's active, graceful presence, His Spirit permeates us with a present hope and with a hope of the final coming of God's Kingdom. For us to be truly human, we must live in self-transcendence. We must live in hope that is grounded in God's concerned and active love for us. The process of created history is under God's providential care, moving to completion in the life to come. The more we can act with full consciousness and reflection, especially through God's revelation in Scripture, the more we can "humanize" ourselves, unleashing the spiritual powers that enable us to transcend this world and pass over to the realm of enduring and limitless spirit.

Only by realizing that our work has lasting value can we truly give ourselves wholly to our "secular" tasks. Unreflective persons, doing their work but not knowing why, also can contribute to the fulfillment of God's universe. But only reflective persons are open to God's graceful communication of Himself in action along with human cooperation. They add a transforming power to the historical process. Teilhard de Chardin gives this practical advice on how to unite the secular and the sacral:

> *Try, with God's help, to perceive the connection — even physical and natural — which binds your labor with the building of the Kingdom of Heaven. . . . Never, at any time, 'whether eating or drinking,'' consent to do anything without first of all realizing its significance and constructive value* in Christo Jesu, *and pursuing it with all your might. This is not simply a commonplace precept for salvation: it is the very path to sanctity for each man according to his state and calling. For what is sanctity in a creature if not to cleave to God with the maximum of his strength? And, what does that maximum cleaving to God mean if not the fulfillment — in the world organized around Christ — of the exact function, be it lowly or eminent, to which that creature is destined both by nature and supernature?*[19]

To have hope for the future so as to work in the present moment is a gift of God's grace. It is ultimately grounded in the cross and resurrection of Jesus Christ whose Spirit convicts us of

God's infinite, self-emptying love which alone conquers sin and death.

The effects of sin and death, obstacles to our hope, include: widespread starvation; the depletion of the world's resources; unequal distribution of economic and political power in societies and between nations; the impersonal nature of technological culture; the loss of community and the breakdown of family life; and, finally, the crisis of faith among believers in a transcendent God, rising out of a self-sufficient scientific and technological culture.[20]

Basis For Christian Hope

Yet before such evils in our world, we Christians bring a luminous hope to the world's darkness:

He has let us know the mystery of his purpose, the hidden plan he so kindly made in Christ from the beginning to act upon when the times had run their course to the end: that he would bring everything together under Christ, as head, everything in the heaven, everything on earth (Ep 1:9-10).

Through our faith that leads us to hope and to living, creative action to cooperate with God's supreme sovereignty, we can discover God in all of His material creation. All of God's creation is penetrated by His immanent presence and active involvement. His grace, as His self-gift to us, is unveiled in the materiality of each historical moment.

God's universal, salvific will to fully develop all creation assures us that there is a unity between His created natures and His grace. As Karl Rahner points out, God's grace is one with human nature and is interwoven with human life and activity.[21] Thus we must not view our world or any creature negatively. We believe that all of creation is *graceful* and open to a personal encounter with God, as grace.

Thus God is not above and outside of our material world. He encounters us in His self-gifting within our everyday world. God is the ground of all being. Touching God's creation, we touch God as actively giving Himself to us in ever-greater transcendence and immanence.

New possibilities open up to us to cooperate with God as co-creators of a better world. Such a better world will be created by greater love and active concern for the good and happiness of others, by the development of human dignity and freedom.

This can only come about if we — in our individual conversion to God, through His forgiving and healing love received in prayerful encounters — become consciously united with God as Triune, loving community.

Love Of Neighbor

Before we can cooperate with God to change the world, we must first extend ourselves toward those nearest us. When we do this, we participate in God's loving action in the world. This is why the Spirit of love is seen in Scripture as a fire. It purifies, it creates out of many elements one new substance unknown before.

Teilhard de Chardin beautifully expresses what Christian hope can do to bring us to the true, transforming power of love:

Some day, after having tamed the ether, the winds, the seas, and gravity, we will capture, for God, the energies of love. And then, for the second time in the history of the World, Man will have discovered Fire.[22]

A Creative Evolution Unto Fullness

We Christians place our hope in Jesus Christ, the Risen Lord, who, even now, is absolute Head of the material created cosmos.

Yet His primacy will not be completely brought about and recognized until His second coming. Then He will return in a mysterious way through the unity among His members, tied in loving obedience to Him, their Head, to lead the created world back to the Father.

No longer will creation be alienated from God. The world will be transfigured; it will become, as St. Paul calls it, a "renovated creation." Our world will not be annihilated, but transfigured. Through the Incarnation, Jesus not only lived upon this material earth, but He began the process of recapitulating all things according to His Father's plan.

Our hope is in the person of Jesus Christ, vibrantly alive, inserted into the material world, actively working with our imperfect cooperation. He is the key to progress and the full meaning of the created cosmos. The whole universe, including the human race, is to be brought into the glorification of God. Jesus Christ is *now* accomplishing in the created universe the completion and fulfillment which His first coming began, and which His second coming will conclude. Yet He turns to us, as the incarnate humility of God the Father and His hidden, kenotic Spirit of love, to invite us to become more involved in creating this New Jerusalem — not up in Heaven, but within the very transcendence locked inside of God's ongoing material creation.

This book's message can best be summed up in the poetic words of Teilhard de Chardin:

> *We must try everything for Christ; we must hope everything for Christ*. Nihil intentatum. *That, on the contrary, is the true Christian attitude. To divinise does not mean to destroy, but to sur-create. We shall never know all that the Incarnation still expects of the world's potentialities. We shall never put enough hope in the growing unity of mankind. . . . The temptations of too large a world, the seductions of too beautiful a world — where are these now? They do not exist.*

Now the earth can certainly clasp me in her giant arms. She can swell me with her life, or draw me back into her dust. She can deck herself with every charm, with every horror, with every mystery. She can intoxicate me with her perfume of tangibility and unity. She can cast me to my knees in expectation of what is maturing in her breast.

But her enchantments can no longer do me harm, since she has become for me, over and above herself, the body of Him who is and of Him who is coming. The divine milieu.[23]

ENDNOTES

1 Emil Brunner: *Man in Revolt* (London: Lutterworth Press, 1939), pp. 97-98.
2 Cf.: Thomas M. Garrett: "Manipulation and Mass Media," in the series: *The Manipulated Man* (The New Concilium, ed. by F. Bockle) (N.Y.: Herder & Herder, 1971), pp. 54-62.
3 Arthur Koestler: *Darkness at Noon*, tr. by Daphne Hardy (N.Y.: Modern Library, 1961).
4 Henri Bergson: *The Two Sources of Morality and Religion*, tr. by R. Ashley Andra and Cloudesley Brereton (Garden City, N.Y.: Doubleday, 1954).
5 Teilhard de Chardin: *The Phenomenon of Man* (N.Y.: Harper & Row, 1965).
6 Jurgen Moltmann: *The Gospel of Liberation*, tr. by H.W. Pipkin (Waco, TX: Word Books, 1973), p. 54.
7 Nicholas Berdyaev: *Slavery and Freedom*, tr. by R.M. French (London: Geoffrey Bles: The Centenary Press, 1943), pp. 252-254.
8 Carl Rogers: *On Becoming a Person* (Boston: Houghton Mifflin, 1961), p. 171.
9 Bernard Loomer, "Dimensions of Freedom," in: *Religious Experience and Process Theology*; ed. Harry James Cargas & Bernard Lee (N.Y. Paulist Press, 1976), p. 325.
10 Carl Rogers: "Learning to be Free," in: *Person to Person, the Problem of Being Human*; ed. C. Rogers, B. Stevens et al. (N.Y.: Pocket Books, Simon & Schuster, Inc., 1971), p. 43.
11 Feodor Dostoevsky: *The Brothers Karamazov*, tr. by Constance Garnett (London: Wm. Heinemann, 1912), pp. 268-269.
12 Scott Peck: *The Road Less Traveled* (N.Y.: Simon & Schuster, 1978), p. 278.
13 Daniel Day Williams: "God and Man," in: *Process Theology: Basic Writings*; ed. E.H. Cousins (N.Y.: Newman Press, 1971), p. 174.
14 Ibid. pp. 182-183.
15 Two modern theologians who present a similar view of grace in contrast to the "scholastic" view of the 13th century which held sway in theological seminaries until Vatican II are: Piet Fransen, S.J.: *Divine Grace and Man*; tr. by Georges Dupont, S.J. (N.Y.: Desclée Co., 1962) and Roger Haigt, S.J.: *The Experience and Language of Grace* (N.Y.: Paulist Press, 1979).

16 Cf.: Karl Rahner: "Nature and Grace," in: *Theological Investigations IV* (Baltimore: Helicon Press, 1966), p. 176.

17 David A. Fleming: "God's Gift and Man's Response," in: *Religious Experience and Process Theology*, p. 224.

18 Dietrich Bonhoeffer: "Thy Kingdom Come," in J.D. Godsey: *Preface to Bonhoeffer* (Philadelphia: Fortress Press, 1965), pp. 28-29.

19 Teilhard de Chardin: *The Divine Milieu* (N.Y.: Harper & Row, 1960), pp. 35-36.

20 Cf.: the more complete list given by Dr. Langdon Gilkey in his draft — published in *Anticipation*, no. 19 (Nov., 1974) by the Division of Church and Society of the World Council of Churches — which he delivered at the Report of the 1974 Conference, held in Bucharest, on *Science and Technology for Human Development: The Ambiguous Future and the Christian Hope*.

21 Karl Rahner: "Concerning the Relationship between Nature and Grace," in: *Theological Investigations I* (Baltimore: Helicon Press, 1961), pp. 297-317. Also on this point, cf.: "Nature and Grace," in: *Theological Investigations IV* (Baltimore: Helicon Press, 1966), pp. 165-188, and "The Order of Redemption within the Order of Creation," in: *The Christian Commitment* (N.Y.: Sheed & Ward, 1963), pp. 38-74.

22 Teilhard de Chardin: "L'Evolution de la Chasteté" (unpublished, written 1934).

23 This is taken from Teilhard de Chardin's epilogue written in Tientsin as the conclusion to *The Divine Milieu*, p. 138.